PRESIDENT'S
TASK FORCE ON
VICTIMS OF CRIME

Task Force Members

Lois Haight Herrington,
Chairman

Garfield Bobo
Frank Carrington
James P. Damos
Doris L. Dolan
Kenneth O. Eikenberry
Robert J. Miller
Reverend Pat Robertson
Stanton E. Samenow

FINAL REPORT   DECEMBER 1982

President's Task Force on Victims of Crime

The Honorable Ronald Reagan
President of the United States
The White House
Washington, D.C.

Dear Mr. President:

When you established the President's Task Force on Victims of Crime on April 23, 1982, you led the nation into a new era in the treatment of victims of crime. Never before has any President recognized the plight of those forgotten by the criminal justice system—the innocent victims of crime.

In meeting the charge that you gave us, we reviewed the available literature on the subject of criminal victimization; we interviewed professionals, both in and out of the criminal justice system, who are responsible for serving victims; and, most importantly, we spoke with citizens from around the country whose lives have been altered by crime.

We found that the perception you shared when you gave us our charge is, unfortunately, true. The innocent victims of crime have been overlooked, their pleas for justice have gone unheeded, and their wounds—personal, emotional, and financial—have gone unattended.

We also found that there is no quick remedy to the innocent victim's plight. Only the sustained efforts of federal, state, and local governments, combined with the resources of the private sector, can restore balance to the criminal justice system.

Citizens from all over the nation told us again and again how heartened they were that this Administration has taken up the challenge, ignored by others in the past, of stopping the mistreatment and neglect of the innocent by those who take liberty for license and by the system of justice itself.

We are pleased to have been able to serve you on this Task Force. We thank you for giving us the privilege of doing so, and we stand ready to assist again should you call upon us in the future.

We have the honor to transmit herewith, pursuant to the provisions of your Executive Order No. 12360, our unanimous recommendations and final report of the President's Task Force on Victims of Crime.

Very truly yours,

Lois Haight Herrington, *Chairman*

Garfield Bobo

Frank Carrington

James P. Damos

Doris L. Dolan

Kenneth O. Eikenberry

Robert J. Miller

Pat Robertson

Stanton E. Samenow

Task Force Staff

Terry Russell, *Executive Director*

Joseph M. Band
Paul L. Knight
William R. McGuiness
Maureen O'Connor
Frank Thorwald
Carol Corrigan,
  Consultant
Elizabeth Harrison,
  Secretary
Patricia J. Wiley,
  Secretary

Acknowledgments

The President's Task Force on Victims of Crime wishes to acknowledge the many persons and organizations who assisted in this study and in the preparation of the final report to the President.

Most especially the Task Force wishes to express gratitude to those victims of crime who came forward, often at the risk of reprisal or embarrassment, to relive their tragedy so that others might learn from it.

We commend those who, despite suffering devastating losses at the hands of criminals, have dedicated their energies and resources to creating organizations to help other crime victims who might experience similar tragedies. Their initiative and strength served as an inspiration to us all.

We also thank Vice President George Bush, Attorney General William French Smith, Counselor to the President Edwin Meese III, the Honorable John Heinz, Senator from the State of Pennsylvania, and the Honorable Paul Laxalt, Senator from the State of Nevada, who gave us the benefit of their insight into this area and who were sources of constant support.

Finally, the Task Force acknowledges the assistance of countless dedicated and concerned citizens throughout the nation, and of the U.S. Marshals Service. We also wish to thank our Executive Director, Terry Russell, and his dedicated staff.

Contents

Statement of The Chairman

If we take the justice out of the criminal justice system we leave behind a system that serves only the criminal.

Something insidious has happened in America: crime has made victims of us all. Awareness of its danger affects the way we think, where we live, where we go, what we buy, how we raise our children, and the quality of our lives as we age. The specter of violent crime and the knowledge that, without warning, any person can be attacked or crippled, robbed, or killed, lurks at the fringes of consciousness. Every citizen of this country is more impoverished, less free, more fearful, and less safe, because of the ever-present threat of the criminal. Rather than alter a system that has proven itself incapable of dealing with crime, society has altered itself.

Every 23 minutes, someone is murdered. Every six minutes a woman is raped. While you read this Statement, two people will be robbed in this country and two more will be shot, stabbed, or seriously beaten. Yet to truly grasp the enormity of the problem those figures must be doubled, because more than 50 percent of violent crime goes unreported. The criminal knows that his risk of punishment is miniscule. A study of four major states revealed that only 9 percent of violent crimes reported were resolved with the perpetrator being incarcerated.

Victims who do survive their attack, and are brave enough to come forward, turn to their government expecting it to do what a good government should—protect the innocent. The American criminal justice system is absolutely dependent on these victims to cooperate. Without the cooperation of victims and witnesses in reporting and testifying about crime, it is impossible in a free society to hold criminals accountable. When victims come forward to perform this vital service, however, they find little protection. They discover instead that they will be treated as appendages of a system appallingly out of balance. They learn that somewhere along the way the system has lost track of the simple truth that it is supposed to be fair and to protect those who obey the law while punishing those who break it. Somewhere along the way, the system began to serve lawyers and judges and defendants, treating the victim with institutionalized disinterest.

The President created this Task Force to address the needs of the millions of Americans and their families who are victimized by crime every year and who often carry its scars into the years to come. He recognized that in the past these victims have pleaded for justice and their pleas have gone unheeded. They have needed help and their needs have gone unattended. The neglect of crime victims is a national disgrace. The President is committed to ending that neglect and to restoring balance to the administration of justice.

This Statement is not followed by a section devoted to statistics. For decades we have been inundated by those grim numbers, yet crime continues to taunt and shatter lives with intolerable frequency. Nor will these remarks be immediately followed by practical proposals, as important as they are and as forcefully as they will be recommended later in this report. Instead, what follows next is a window into the victim's experience. The Task Force strongly urges you to read it before you go further. You cannot appreciate the victim problem if you approach it solely with your intellect. The intellect rebels.

The important proposals contained here will not be clear unless you first confront the human reality of victimization. Few are willing to do so. Unless you are, however, you will not be able to understand. During our hearings we were told by one eloquent witness, "It is hard not to turn away from victims. Their pain is discomforting; their anger is sometimes embarrassing; their mutilations are upsetting." Victims are vital reminders of our own vulnerability. But one cannot turn away.

You must know what it is to have your life wrenched and broken, to realize that you will never really be the same. Then you must experience what it means to survive, only to be blamed and used and ignored by those you thought were there to help you. Only when you are willing to confront all these things will you understand what victimization means.

We who have served on this Task Force have been forever changed by the victims we have met, by the experiences they have shared, by the wisdom sprung from suffering that they imparted. What we heard from these forgotten citizens is the basis for the following section, which gives an overview of the variety of problems faced by victims at every stage of their experience. The problems we refer to unfortunately exist. They exist in every jurisdiction of the country. The examples used in this report to illustrate these problems are taken directly from victim testimony. While not every victim will face every one of these problems, our inquiry has shown that almost every victim will face some of them.

The lessons of the victims run like a thread throughout and are the foundation of all the proposals that follow. Please take the time to learn, as we have, the depth and the human aspect of this grave social problem, then join in seeking and implementing the solutions.

Lois Haight Herrington
Chairman

Washington, D.C.
December 20, 1982

Victims of Crime
in America

Victims of Crime in America

Before you, the reader, can appreciate the necessity of changing the way victims are treated, you must confront the essential reality that almost all Americans, at some time in their lives, will be touched by crime. Among the most difficult obstacles are the myths that if people are wise, virtuous, and cautious, they will escape, and that those who are victimized are somehow responsible for their fate. These are pernicious falsehoods. First, for every person mugged on a dark street at 3 a.m., many more are terrorized in their homes, schools, offices, or on main thoroughfares in the light of day. Second, to adopt the attitude of victim culpability is to accept that citizens have lost the right to walk their streets safely regardless of the hour or locale; it is to abandon these times and places to be claimed as the hunting preserves of the lawless.

When I wanted to talk about my son, I soon found that murder is a taboo subject in our society. I found, to my surprise, that nice people apparently just don't get killed.—a victim's mother

Violent crime honors no sanctuary. It strikes when least expected, often when the victim is doing the most commonplace things. Victims testified at hearings of the President's Task Force on Victims of Crime about these occurrences:

- As she walks across campus on her first afternoon at college, a young woman is murdered.
- A pharmacist turns to wait on a customer and is confronted by a robber wearing a ski mask.
- A child is molested by the driver of his school bus.
- A man answers the front door and is shot in the chest.
- As a mother shops in a department store, her child, looking at books an aisle away, is kidnapped.
- Walking down the street at lunchtime, an elderly man is assaulted from behind and left permanently blind.
- While a woman is leaving a shopping center someone jumps into her car; 5 hours of rape and torture follow.

To blame victims for crime is like analyzing the cause of World War II and asking, "What was Pearl Harbor doing in the Pacific, anyway?—a victim

- An elderly woman's purse is snatched and she is thrown to the ground, suffering injuries that prevent her from walking again.
- In the restroom of a hotel, a woman is raped by an attacker who is hiding in an adjoining stall.
- A couple returning home from work opens the door to discover that the house has been ransacked.
- A cabdriver, working in the afternoon, turns to collect a fare and is shot.

Based on the testimony of these and other victims, we have drawn a composite of a victim of crime in America today. This victim is every victim; she could be you or related to you.

If a totally innocent young man can be shot to death, if my son can die with no guilt or no blame, then your son can, too. Because this is unacceptable to people, they refuse to accept it.—a victim's father

II

You are a 50-year-old woman living alone. You are asleep one night when suddenly you awaken to find a man standing over you with a knife at your throat. As you start to scream, he beats and cuts you. He then rapes you. While you watch helplessly, he searches the house, taking your jewelry, other valuables, and money. He smashes furniture and windows in a display of senseless violence. His rampage ended, he rips out the telephone line, threatens you again, and disappears into the night.

He said, "Move or yell and I'll kill you." I didn't doubt his word.—a victim

At least, you have survived. Terrified, you rush to the first lighted house on the block. While you wait for the police, you pray that your attacker was bluffing when he said he'd return if you called them. Finally, what you expect to be help arrives.

The police ask questions, take notes, dust for fingerprints, make photographs. When you tell them you were raped, they take you to the hospital. Bleeding from cuts, your front teeth knocked out, bruised and in pain, you are told that your wounds are superficial, that rape itself is not considered an injury. Awaiting treatment, you sit alone for hours, suffering the stares of curious passersby. You feel dirty, bruised, disheveled, and abandoned. When your turn comes for examination, the intern seems irritated because he has been called out to treat you. While he treats you, he says that he hates to get involved in rape cases because he doesn't like going to court. He asks if you "knew the man you had sex with."

The nurse says she wouldn't be out alone at this time of night. It seems pointless to explain that the attacker broke into your house and had a knife. An officer says you must go through this process, then the hospital sends you a bill for the examination that the investigators insisted upon. They give you a box filled with test tubes and swabs and envelopes and tell you to hold onto it. They'll run some tests if they ever catch your rapist.

Finally, you get home somehow, in a cab you paid for and wearing a hospital gown because they took your clothes as evidence. Everything that the attacker touched seems soiled. You're afraid to be in your house alone. The one place where you were always safe, at home, is sanctuary no longer. You are afraid to remain, yet terrified to leave your home unprotected.

You didn't realize when you gave the police your name and address that it would be given to the press and to the defendant through the police reports. Your friends call to say they saw this information in the paper, your picture on television. You haven't yet absorbed what's happened to you when you get calls from insurance companies and firms that sell security devices. But these calls pale in comparsion to the threats that come from the defendant and his friends.

You're astonished to discover that your attacker has been arrested, yet while in custody he has free and unmonitored access to a phone. He can threaten you from jail. The judge orders him not to annoy you, but when the phone calls are brought to his attention, the judge does nothing.

At least you can be assured that the man who attacked you is in custody, or so you think. No one tells you when he is released on his promise to come to court. No one ever asks you if you've been threatened. The judge is never told that the defendant said he'd kill you if you told or that he'd get even if he went to jail. Horrified, you ask how he got out after what he did. You're told the judge can't consider whether he'll be dangerous, only whether he'll come back to court. He's been accused and convicted before, but he always come to court; so he must be released.

At first, opening a drawer that had been emptied on that day started tears to flow.—a victim

Before my assailants left, they robbed us of all our grocery money and repeated their threat to kill me and my children if I reported them to the police.—a victim

One morning I woke up, looked out my bedroom window and saw the man who had assaulted me standing across the street staring at me. I thought he was in jail.—a victim

You learn only by accident that he's at large; this discovery comes when you turn a corner and confront him. He knows where you live. He's been there. Besides, your name and address were in the paper and in the reports he's seen. Now nowhere is safe. He watches you from across the street; he follows you on the bus. Will he come back in the night? What do you do? Give up your home? Lose your job? Assume a different name? Get your mail at the post office? Carry a weapon? Even if you wanted to, could you afford to do these things?

You try to return to normal. You don't want to talk about what happened, so you decide not to tell your co-workers about the attack. A few days go by and the police unexpectedly come to your place of work. They show their badges to the receptionist and ask to see you. They want you to look at some photographs, but they don't explain that to your co-workers. You try to explain later that you're the victim, not the accused.

The phone rings and the police want you to come to a line-up. It may be 1:00 a.m. or in the middle of your work day, but you have to go; the suspect and his lawyer are waiting. It will not be the last time you are forced to conform your life to their convenience. You appear at the police station and the line-up begins. The suspect's lawyer sits next to you, but he does not watch the stage; he stares at you. It will not be the last time you must endure his scrutiny.

It took me a long time to get my 8-year-old daughter to sleep that night, but finally I did. Later I got a call that the molester had been arrested, and that my daughter and I had to go down to a police line-up at 1:00 a.m. We did go, but it was very traumatic for her.—a victim's mother

III

You have lived through the crime and made it through the initial investigation. They've caught the man who harmed you, and he's been charged with armed burglary, robbery, and rape. Now he'll be tried. Now you expect justice.

You receive a subpoena for a preliminary hearing. No one tells you what it will involve, how long it will take, or how you should prepare. You assume that this is the only time you will have to appear. But you are only beginning your initiation in a system that will grind away at you for months, disrupt your life, affect your emotional stability, and certainly cost you money; it may cost you your job, and, for the dura-

I will never forget being raped, kidnapped, and robbed at gunpoint. However, my sense of disillusionment of the judicial system is many times more painful. I could not in good faith urge anyone to participate in this hellish process.—a victim

tion, will prevent you from putting the crime behind you and reconstructing your life.

Before the hearing, a defense investigator comes to talk to you. When he contacts you, he says he's "investigating your case," and that he "works for the county." You assume, as he intends you to, that he's from the police or the prosecutor's office. Only after you give him a statement do you discover that he works for the man who attacked you.

This same investigator may visit your neighbors and co-workers, asking questions about you. He discusses the case with them, always giving the defendant's side. Suddenly, some of the people who know you seem to be taking a different view of what happened to you and why.

It's the day of the hearing. You've never been to court before, never spoken in public. You're very nervous. You rush to arrive at 8 a.m. to talk to a prosecutor you've never met. You wait in a hallway with a number of other witnesses. It's now 8:45. Court starts at 9:00. No one has spoken to you. Finally, a man sticks his head out a door, calls out your name, and asks, "Are you the one who was raped?" You're aware of the stares as you stand and suddenly realize that this is the prosecutor, the person you expect will represent your interests.

You only speak to the prosecutor for a few minutes. You ask to read the statement you gave to the police but he says there isn't time. He asks you some questions that make you wonder if he's read it himself. He asks you other questions that make you wonder if he believes it.

The prosecutor tells you to sit on the bench outside the courtroom. Suddenly you see the man who raped you coming down the hall. No one has told you he would be here. He's with three friends. He points you out. They all laugh and jostle you a little as they pass. The defendant and two friends enter the courtroom; one friend sits on the bench across from you and stares. Suddenly, you feel abandoned, alone, afraid. Is this what it's like to come to court and seek justice?

You sit on that bench for an hour, then two. You don't see the prosecutor, he has disappeared into the courtroom. Finally, at noon he comes out and says, "Oh, you're still here? We continued that case to next month."

You repeat this process many times before you actually testify at the preliminary hearing. Each time you go to court, you hire a babysitter or take leave from work, pay for parking, wait for hours, and finally are told to go home. No one ever asks if the new dates are convenient to you. You miss vacations and medical appointments. You use up sick leave and vacation days to make your court appearances. Your employer is losing his patience. Every time you are gone his business is disrupted. But you are fortunate. If you were new at your job, or worked part-time, or didn't have an understanding boss, you could lose your job. Many victims do.

The preliminary hearing was an event for which your were completely unprepared. You learn later than the defense is often harder on a victim at the preliminary hearing than during the trial. In trial, the defense attorney cannot risk alienating the jury. At this hearing, there is only the judge—and he certainly doesn't seem concerned about you. One of the first questions you are asked is where you live. You finally moved after your attack; you've seen the defendant and his friends, and you're terrified of having them know where you now live. When you explain that you'd be happy to give your old address, the judge says he'll dismiss the case or hold you in contempt of court if you don't answer the question. The prosecutor says nothing. During your testimony, you are also compelled to say where you work, how you get there, and what your schedule is.

Hours later you are released from the stand after reliving your attack in public, in intimate detail. You have been made to feel completely powerless. As you sat facing a smirking defendant and as you described his threats, you were accused of lying and inviting the "encounter." You have cried in front of these uncaring strangers. As you leave no one thanks you. When you get back to work they ask what took you so long.

It takes a lot of nerve to get up on the stand and testify against somebody who has a habit of shooting and stabbing people and then getting back on the street again, you know.—a victim

You are stunned when you later learn that the defendant also raped five others; one victim was an 8-year-old girl. During her testimony she was asked to describe her attacker's anatomy. Spectators laughed when she said she did not understand the words being used. When she was asked to draw a picture of her attacker's genitalia the girl fled from the courtroom and ran sobbing to her mother, who had been subpoenaed by the defense and had to wait outside. The youngster was forced to sit alone and recount, as you did, each minute of the attack. You know how difficult it was for you to speak of these things; you cannot imagine how it was for a child.

Now the case is scheduled for trial. Again there are delays. When you call and ask to speak with the prosecutor, you are told the case has been reassigned. You tell your story in detail to five different prosecutors before the case is tried. Months go by and no one tells you what's happening. Periodically you are subpoenaed to appear. You leave your work, wait, and are finally told to go home.

If we invested our money the way we ask victims to invest their time we'd all go broke.—Deborah Kelly

Continuances are granted because the courts are filled, one of the lawyers is on another case, the judge has a meeting to attend or an early tennis match. You can't understand why they couldn't have discovered these problems before you came to court. When you ask if the next date could be set a week later so you can attend a family gathering out of state, you are told that the defendant has the right to a speedy trial. You stay home from the reunion and the case is continued.

The defense attorney continues to call. Will you change your story? Don't you want to drop the charges?

Time passes and you hear nothing. Your property is not returned. You learn that there are dozens of defense motions that can be filed before the trial. If denied, many of them can be appealed. Each motion, each court date means a new possibility for delay. If the defendant is out of custody and fails to come to court, nothing can happen until he is reapprehended. If he is successful in avoiding recapture, the case may be so compromised by months or years of delay that a successful prosecution is impossible. For as long as the case drags on, your life is on hold. You don't want to start a new assignment at work or move to a new city because you know that at any time the round of court appearances may begin again. The wounds of your attack will never heal as long as you know that you will be asked to relive those horrible moments.

No one tells you anything about the progress of the case. You want to be involved, consulted, and informed, but prosecutors often plea bargain without consulting victims. You're afraid someone will let the defendant plead guilty to a lesser charge and be sentenced to probation. You meet another victim at court who tells you that she and her family were kidnapped and her children molested. Even though the prosecutor assured her that he would not accept a plea bargain, after talking with the attorneys in his chambers, the judge allowed the defendant to plead as charged with the promise of a much-reduced sentence. You hope that this won't happen in your case.

Why didn't anyone consult me? I was the one who was kidnapped, not the State of Virginia.—a victim

IV

Finally the day of trial arrives. It is 18 months since you were attacked. You've been trying for a week to prepare yourself. It is painful to dredge up the terror again, but you know that the outcome depends on you; the prosecutor has told you that the way you behave will make or break the case. You can't get too angry on the stand because then the jury might not like you. You can't break down and sob because then you will appear too emotional, possibly unstable. In addition to the tremendous pressure of having to relive the horrible details of the crime, you're expected to be an actress as well.

You go to court. The continuances are over; the jury has been selected. You sit in a waiting room with the defendant's family and friends. Again you feel threatened, vulnerable, and alone.

You expect the trial to be a search for the truth; you find that it is a performance orchestrated by lawyers and the judge, with the jury hearing only half the facts. The defendant was found with your watch in his pocket. The judge has suppressed this evidence because the officer who arrested him didn't have a warrant.

Your character is an open subject of discussion and innuendo. The defense is allowed to question you on incidents going back to your childhood. The jury is never told that the defendant has two prior convictions for the same offense and has been to prison three times for other crimes. You sought help from a counselor to deal with the shattering effect of this crime on your life. You told him about your intimate

It is almost impossible to walk into a courtroom and describe in detail the thing you most want to forget. It is also devastating to have to face your assailant. Although you are surrounded by people and deputies of the court, the fear is still overwhelming.—a victim

To be a victim at the hands of the criminal is an unforgettable nightmare. But to then become a victim at the hands of the criminal justice system is an unforgivable travesty. It makes the criminal and the criminal justice system partners in crime.—Robert Grayson

fears and feelings. Now he has been called by the defense and his notes and records have been subpoenaed.

My daughter dreaded the confrontation with the man at trial. How would she react when she had to sit near him, walk by him, look at him?—a victim's mother

You are on the stand for hours. The defense does its best to make you appear a liar, a seductress, or both. You know you cannot relax for a moment. Don't answer unless you understand the question. Don't be embarrassed when everyone seems angry because you do not understand. Think ahead. Be responsive. Don't volunteer. Don't get tired.

Finally you are finished with this part of the nightmare. You would like to sit and listen to the rest of the trial but you cannot. You're a witness and must wait outside. The jury will decide the outcome of one of the major events of your life. You cannot hear the testimony that will guide their judgment.

The verdict is guilty. You now look to the judge to impose a just sentence.

V

You expect the sentence to reflect how terrible the crime was. You ask the prosecutor how this decision is reached, and are told that once a defendant is convicted he is interviewed at length by a probation officer. He gives his side of the story, which may be blatantly false in light of the proven facts. A report that delves into his upbringing, family relationships, education, physical and mental health, and employment and conviction history is prepared. The officer will often speak to the defendant's relatives and friends. Some judges will send the defendant to a facility where a complete psychiatric and sociological work-up is prepared. You're amazed that no one will ever ask you about the crime, or the effect it has had on you and your family. You took the defendant's blows, heard his threats, listened to him brag that he'd "beat the rap" or "con the judge." No one ever hears of these things. They never give you the chance to tell them.

The judge told me I should not be too mad at the man who molested my daughter—after all, the rape was not completed.—a victim's mother

At sentencing, the judge hears from the defendant, his lawyer, his mother, his minister, his friends. You learn by chance what day the hearing was. When you do attend, the defense attorney says you're vengeful and it's apparent that you overreacted to being raped and robbed because you chose to come and see the sentencing. You ask permission to address the judge and are told that you are not allowed to do so.

The judge sentences your attacker to three years in prison, less than one year for every hour he kept you in pain and terror. That seems very lenient to you. Only later do you discover that he'll probably serve less than half of his actual sentence in prison because of good-time and work-time credits that are given to him immediately. The man who broke into your home, threatened to slit your throat with a knife, and raped, beat, and robbed you will be out of custody in less than 18 months. You are not told when he will actually be released, and you are not allowed to attend the parole release hearing anyway.

The man who strangled my daughter to death will only serve four years.—a victim's father

VI

For this victim the ordeal of the trial is over, but the ordeal of being a victim is far from over; it continues with unrelenting pressure. The consequences for the victim described in this essay were found by the Task Force to be very real and very commonplace. Even at the point of conviction of the defendant, the system can place new burdens on the victim; if the defendant wins an appeal, the victim may have to go through the trial process all over again. There might have been more than one defendant, or one might have been a juvenile. This would have meant two or three trials, two or three times as many court appearances and hours of cross-examination, double or triple the harassment. There might have been two or three law enforcement agencies involved in the case who did not cooperate with each other. The defendant's every right has been protected, and now he serves his time in a public facility, receiving education at public expense. In a few months his sentence will have run. Victims receive sentences too; their sentences may be life long.

If you were the victim, you may now be crippled or blind as a result of brutality. You may have lost a limb and may have to undergo surgery repeatedly to repair the body your attacker nearly destroyed. You were active, healthy, full of life; now you may be dependent and destitute.

The economic impact on you can be devastating. You may have been hospitalized and unable to return

I'm a senior citizen but I never considered myself old. I was active, independent. Now I live in a nursing home and sit in a wheelchair. The day I was mugged was the day I began to die.—a victim

to work for months, if ever. You may have used all your sick leave and vacation. You may need braces, a wheelchair, a ramp to get into your home, a hearing aid, or a special bed. You may not be able to afford them, because you may well be in debt. You may have lost what it took you years to build. You may have lost what you treasured most—the locket with your mother's picture that can never be replaced. Your business may be bankrupt, or you may have run through your savings. Your once excellent credit rating may now be gone.

You may have to leave your home. If you can not leave, you may no longer feel safe there; you may no longer be able to sleep in the room where you were raped. Every time you open your door you may feel anew the sense of invasion.

Being a crime victim adds a new dimension to the definition of self.—Morton Bard

The psychological scars are perhaps the hardest to bear. These are the hardships that those untouched by crime find the most difficult to understand. Before the crime you felt reasonably safe and secure; the world is now a violent and deadly place to you. It seems you must either accept guilt for what happened to you or condemn yourself to the realization that you have no control. Everything seems to reinforce these feelings of inadequacy. Doctors dictate part of your days; lawyers and creditors dominate the rest. You may sleep badly, eat poorly, be continually afraid, depressed, ill. The most mundane occurrences make you flash back to the crime. Before the crime you were bright, attractive, talented, competent; now you may feel as though you are none of these. The criminal has taken from you your sense of security, your sense of humor, your sense of self. You are fearful and you are angry.

The general feeling of being a living victim or victim-survivor is one of an outcast. Ostracized from society, forgotten by family, friends, fellow workers. No one, or very few, bring the subject up.—a victim

You may well be isolated in your anguish. You can't believe that this could happen to you. Others want to believe that the aftermath is not as bad as you claim. If it should happen to them, they could handle it better, be stronger, recover sooner. You have become a shadow of their own vulnerability. They must deny you. So they tell you that your anger, your desire for justice, your suspicion and fear are unreasonable. But when you are beaten and robbed, your home destroyed, or your husband or child murdered, who has standing to label your anger irrational?

Many people can accept tragedy that comes through natural disaster or accident, but you know that your victimization was intentional. They say that by now you should be back to normal. But they don't have to see your scars in the mirror every morning. The court system doesn't call them once a month for years to dredge it all up again.

A family that was once happy and close-knit all of a sudden is no longer complete.— a victim

Having survived all this, you reflect on how you and your victimizer are treated by the system that is called justice. You are aware of inequities that are more than merely procedural. During trial and after sentencing the defendant had a free lawyer; he was fed and housed; given physical and psychiatric treatment, job training, education, support for his family, counsel on appeal. Although you do not oppose any of these safeguards, you realize that you have helped to pay for all these benefits for the criminal. Now, in addition and by yourself, you must try to repair all that his crime has destroyed; and what you cannot repair, you must endure.

How can the system have gotten this far away from what it is supposed to be?—a victim

Recommendations for Government Action

Recommendations for Government Action

The United States is a nation of laws. If laws are to be obeyed, they must be respected; to be respected, they must be just. A system that fails to be equitable cannot survive. The system was designed to be the fairest in history, but it has lost the balance that has been the cornerstone of its wisdom.

Proposed Executive and Legislative Action at the Federal and State Levels

The legislative and executive branches, at both the state and federal level, must pass and enforce laws that protect all citizens and that recognize society's interest in assisting the innocent to recover from victimization. The recommendations that follow comprise proposals for action by both federal and state executives and legislatures.

Recommendations for Federal and State Action

1. Legislation should be proposed and enacted to ensure that addresses of victims and witnesses are not made public or available to the defense, absent a clear need as determined by the court.

2. Legislation should be proposed and enacted to ensure that designated victim counseling is legally privileged and not subject to defense discovery or subpoena.

3. Legislation should be proposed and enacted to ensure that hearsay is admissible and sufficient in preliminary hearings, so that victims need not testify in person.

4. Legislation should be proposed and enacted to amend the bail laws to accomplish the following:

   a. Allow courts to deny bail to persons found by clear and convincing evidence to present a danger to the community;

   b. Give the prosecution the right to expedited appeal of adverse bail determinations, analogous to the right presently held by the defendant;

   c. Codify existing case law defining the authority of the court to detain defendants as to whom no conditions of release are adequate to ensure appearance at trial;

   d. Reverse, in the case of serious crimes, any standard that presumptively favors release of convicted persons awaiting sentence or appealing their convictions;

   e. Require defendants to refrain from criminal activity as a mandatory condition of release; and

   f. Provide penalties for failing to appear while released on bond or personal recognizance that are more closely proportionate to the penalties for the offense with which the defendant was originally charged.

5. Legislation should be proposed and enacted to abolish the exclusionary rule as it applies to Fourth Amendment issues.

6. Legislation should be proposed and enacted to open parole release hearings to the public.

7. Legislation should be proposed and enacted to abolish parole and limit judicial discretion in sentencing.

8. Legislation should be proposed and enacted to require that school officials report violent offenses against students or teachers, or the possession of weapons or narcotics on school grounds. The knowing failure to make such a report to the police, or deterring others from doing so, should be designated a misdemeanor.

9. Legislation should be proposed and enacted to make available to businesses and organizations the sexual assault, child molestation, and pornography arrest records of prospective and present employees whose work will bring them in regular contact with children.

10. Legislation should be proposed and enacted to accomplish the following:
    a. Require victim impact statements at sentencing;
    b. Provide for the protection of victims and witnesses from intimidation;
    c. Require restitution in all cases, unless the court provides specific reasons for failing to require it;
    d. Develop and implement guidelines for the fair treatment of crime victims and witnesses; and
    e. Prohibit a criminal from making any profit from the sale of the story of his crime. Any proceeds should be used to provide full restitution to his victims, pay the expenses of his prosecution, and finally, assist the crime victim compensation fund.

11. Legislation should be proposed and enacted to establish or expand employee assistance programs for victims of crime employed by government.

12. Legislation should be proposed and enacted to ensure that sexual assault victims are not requried to assume the cost of physical examinations and materials used to obtain evidence.

Commentary

Executive and Legislative Recommendation 1:
Legislation should be proposed and enacted to ensure that addresses of victims and witnesses are not made public or available to the defense, absent a clear need as determined by the court.

Victims and witnesses share a common, often justified apprehension that they and members of their family will be threatened or harassed as a result of their testimony against a violent criminal. This fear is quite understandable. Victims and witnesses have seen personally what the defendant is capable of doing. In addition, threats and actual retaliation are not uncommon.

Fear of defendant reprisal manifests itself in a number of ways, all of which are extremely detrimental to the safety of the community. First, it is a factor in the decision of many victims not to report a crime. Second, it may cause many victims and witnesses to choose not to cooperate in the investigation or trial of a case. It is unfair to subject those courageous enough to appear and testify truthfully to months or even years of living in fear for their own safety or that of their family.

Although this fear cannot be eliminated, it can be mitigated by keeping the home addresses and phone numbers of victims and witnesses private. At the outset, there is no reason why police or prosecutors should release this information to the news media. Both agencies should take steps to ensure that this release does not occur. If jurisdictions require that certain police reports be open to the public, they should either amend their statutes or redesign their forms so that this information is not available for publication.

Likewise, home addresses should not be given to the defense in the absence of judicial determination of a need that overrides the victim's need for security. This issue first arises when defense counsel demands pre-trial discovery of the victim's and witnesses' home addresses in order to interview them. In jurisdictions where defense counsel has the right to contact prosecution witnesses before trial, prosecutors should arrange for contact in government offices, rather than release the address of a witness. Current legislation that requires release of addresses should be amended.

Seniors don't report crimes to the police because they are afraid that the defendants who mugged them the first time will come back and beat them up even more seriously because they went to the police.—a victim

The next morning there was another account in the paper, this time with not only my name, but my mother's and daughter's name as well as our ages, and our exact address.—a victim

I was upset when I was asked about my new location where I lived, and when I had to give my children's names, the man who had caused these problems was sitting in the courtroom and I was telling him how he or someone else could find me.—a victim

This experience brought me closer to death than one could ever imagine, not only because of the gun, but because of the rape itself. I felt ashamed, and I thought I wanted to die. My heart felt like it was going to burst. Crying and talking with people I could trust helped to relieve the pressures. I needed to share feelings with people who would keep my secret for however long I needed them to.—a victim

When victims or witnesses testify, they are frequently asked for their home address, sometimes by the prosecutor. Prosecutors should stop soliciting this sensitive information and should object to defense efforts to obtain it. Only when the defense is able to establish that the address is clearly relevant to credibility or to the facts of the case should the question be allowed.

**Executive and Legislative Recommendation 2:
Legislation should be proposed and enacted to ensure that designated victim counseling is legally privileged and not subject to defense discovery or subpoena.**

A number of organizations and victim/witness units provide psychological crisis counseling to ease the real and profound psychological trauma of victimization. Since the development of rape crisis centers, the need for and benefits derived from counseling for rape victims has become well established. Testimony before the Task Force confirms that counseling is necessary for many violent crime victims as well as their families. Such counseling has proven extremely beneficial and should be strongly encouraged at all levels.

Although some centers have made psychiatrists or psychologists available, the vast majority of the work has been done by social workers, nurses, or by people who have been victims themselves. During the counseling process, victims speak of their fears and feelings arising from the crime; these reactions are often related to their personal history and psychological makeup.

Failure to extend confidentiality to crisis counseling incurs the risk of undermining the effectiveness of the counseling. Some victims who need this kind of help now fear to seek it. Without the protection of confidentiality, victims have found their files subpoenaed by the defense, and feel betrayed when thoughts and feelings that they considered private are opened to public scrutiny in a courtroom.

Statutes that were passed before the importance of victim counseling became recognized extend confidentiality only to counseling by psychologists and psychiatrists. These statutes protect only those who can afford private treatment by these professionals; they do not shield the vast majority of victims.

At least one state has enacted a statute making rape victims' communications to counselors legally privileged.[1] While this is a step in the right direction, we believe that the privilege should encompass the counseling of all crime victims. Because of the responsibility of the prosecutor to afford discovery to the defendant, it is not contemplated that this counseling privilege extend to the prosecutor's office.

It was a great relief to have someone to talk to, who would in no way pass onto others what I thought, felt, or did at that confusing time.—a victim

Executive and Legislative Recommendation 3:
Legislation should be proposed and enacted to ensure that hearsay is admissible and sufficient in preliminary hearings, so that victims need not testify in person.

Victims of crime are frequently required to come to court time after time in connection with a single case. Separate appearances are often required for the initial charging of the case, preliminary hearing, and grand jury testimony, in addition to repeated appearances for pre-trial conferences and the trial itself. The penalty for the victim's failure to appear at any court proceeding is usually dismissal of the case.

Requiring the victim to appear and testify at a preliminary hearing is an enormous imposition that can be eliminated. A preliminary hearing, as used in this context, is an initial judicial examination into the facts and circumstances of a case to determine if sufficient evidence for further prosecution exists. It should not be a mini-trial, lasting hours, days, or even weeks, in which the victim has to relive his victimization. In some cases, the giving of such testimony is simply impossible within the time constraints imposed. Within a few days of the crime, some victims are still hospitalized or have been so traumatized that they are unable to speak about their experience. Because the victim cannot attend the hearing, it does not take place, and the defendant is often free to terrorize others.

It should be sufficient for this determination that the police officer or detective assigned to the case testify as to the facts, with the defendant possessing the right of cross-examination. The defendant's right to pre-trial discovery of the government's case outside the courtroom and pursuant to local rules would remain intact. The sufficiency of hearsay at a preliminary hearing is firmly established in the federal courts, as well as in a number of local jurisdictions.

Executive and Legislative Recommendation 4:
Legislation should be proposed and enacted to amend the bail laws to accomplish the following:

   a. **Allow courts to deny bail to persons found by clear and convincing evidence to present a danger to the community;**
   b. **Give the prosecution the right to expedited appeal of adverse bail determinations, analogous to the right presently held by the defendant;**
   c. **Codify existing case law defining the authority of the court to detain defendants as to whom no conditions of release are adequate to ensure appearance at trial;**
   d. **Reverse, in the case of serious crimes, any standard that presumptively favors release of convicted persons awaiting sentence or appealing their convictions;**
   e. **Require defendants to refrain from criminal activity as a mandatory condition of release; and**
   f. **Provide penalties for failing to appear while released on bond or personal recognizance that are more closely proportionate to the penalties for the offense with which the defendant was orginally charged.**

The imbalance between the legitimate and necessary interest of the victim in protection and the interest of the accused in procedural safeguards is most apparent in the area of bail. A substantial proportion of the crimes committed in this country are committed by defendants who have beeen released on bail or their own recognizance.[2]

The legal system exists to protect both the accused and the community. However, the bail system, as it currently operates in many jurisdictions, addresses only the protection of the defendant, and completely ignores the victims. To be just, a system must be devised that serves the rightful needs of both.

Victims of violent crime have expressed with outrage and indignation their dissatisfaction with bail laws in many jurisdictions. Victims who have been robbed or raped, and the families of those murdered by persons who were released on bail while facing serious charges and possessing a prior record of violence, simply cannot understand why these persons were free to harm them. When that same person is again released and returns to threaten or intimidate, these victims frequently lose all faith in a justice system so obviously unable to protect them.

In deciding issues of bail, the court must have the authority to balance the defendant's interest in remaining free on a charge of which he is presumed innocent with the reality that many defendants have proven, by their conviction records, that they have committed and are likely to commit crimes while at large. The authority for such consideration does not now exist in many jurisdictions. In federal courts and in many state courts, the only question that can be addressed at a bail hearing is whether the defendant will appear for his court dates.[3] Such a policy is both foolish and shortsighted.

This Task Force is not alone in its recommendation that the danger that a defendant poses must be considered in ruling on bail decisions. The U.S. Congress, the American Bar Association, the National Conference on Commissioners on Uniform State Laws, and the Attorney General's Task Force on Violent Crime have all reached a similar conclusion.

Several of the recommendations set forth above are self-explanatory. Two of them, however, *c* and *e,* require further elaboration.

c. Each defendant must be evaluated individually in terms of the threat he poses and the likelihood of his returning to court. In most jurisdictions a body of case law has arisen that mandates the consideration of such factors as a defendant's ties to the community in terms of family, housing, employment, and other responsibilities. Another noteworthy factor is the defendant's access to wealth, alternative residence sites, and long-range transportation. An accused drug dealer who has foreign bank accounts and owns both his own plane and a villa in a country that will not extradite him would not appear to be a good bail risk even on a relatively high bond. Codification of case law authorizing consideration of such factors would ensure consistency in their application.

e. Courts must require that defendants not commit new crimes while on bail. To do otherwise creates a

*A man was convicted in 1974 of sexually assaulting a child. He repeated the offense, and in 1980 was convicted again, and sentenced to 18 months. He served seven months. After that conviction, he was arrested again for molesting a 7-year-old. He was released on bail, and while out on bail, he molested yet another child.—
Bea McPherson*

revolving-door approach to crime. Any new arrest, with a finding of probable cause, should result in the swift revocation of bail or personal recognizance release on the original charge.

Court orders that are not enforced are meaningless. Not only do they fail in attaining their goals, they also teach that lawful orders can be violated with impunity. Such an attitude cannot be tolerated. Courts should not reinforce it by failing to take effective action.

Our recommendations on bail are, with some modifications, a reaffirmation of the recommendations of the Attorney General's Task Force on Violent Crime. Because those earlier recommendations have not yet been enacted into law, we wish to add the often-forgotten but eloquent voices of victims to the demand for needed change. The Task Force on Violent Crime limited its bail recommendations to federal law, noting that pre-trial delays in some states were too long to keep defendants incarcerated without an adjudication of guilt. We share their concern, but we do intend our recommendations to apply to states because of the cost to victims, who suffer long pre-trial delays before they can finally attempt to put the ordeal of their victimization behind them and resume a normal life with the knowledge that justice has been achieved. This is one of the reasons for our recommendation, presented elsewhere in this report, that the problem of multiple continuances and pre-trial delay, and the reasons for that delay, be remedied.

**Executive and Legislative Recommendation 5:
Legislation should be proposed and enacted to abolish the exclusionary rule as it applies to Fourth Amendment issues.**

It should be reiterated that this Task Force in no way seeks to diminish the important protections extended to all citizens by the Fourth Amendment. The right to freedom from unreasonable search and seizure is one of the pillars of American liberty. It is not this goal of liberty that must be reexamined, but the detrimental way the system has sought to pursue it.

There is no right stated in the Constitution to the exclusion of seized evidence, any more than there is a right to break the law with impunity. Anyone evaluating the exclusionary rule must constantly keep this basic premise in mind. The framers of the Constitution did not create the exclusionary rule for violations of the Fourth Amendment. They could have done so. They did in the Fifth Amendment, which clearly provides that information forcefully taken from a suspect cannot be used against him. This constitutional adoption of the exclusionary principle was specifically not relied upon in setting out the Fourth Amendment. The exclusionary rule is instead a judicially created rule of procedure that fails to serve the goals it seeks, and fails at a tremendous cost.

The rule is an idea that began with a lofty and necessary premise, the protection of citizens from improper state action. The rule provides, essentially, that any evidence discovered as a result of improper police action will be inadmissible at trial. The idea is that punishing the police will curb misconduct. But the experience of almost 70 years at the federal level and more than 20 years at the state level has shown that courts are not at all clear on what they consider to be misconduct; the rule does not deter police—instead, the rule punishes the innocent victim and all law-abiding citizens by preventing effective prosecution; and the court decisions interpreting the Fourth Amendment have created an incredibly complex body of law, and it is unfair to punish a victim because a police officer acting under exigent circumstances made the wrong decision. If all the bases for the rule are unfounded, why then does it remain in effect?

Great emotion is generated in any discussion of the rule because its proponents treat the rule itself with the same sanctity as the rights it purports to protect. Unlawful government intrusion is like disease; no one is in favor of it. It must be remembered that the exclusionary rule is a remedy only, and not a very good one. It thus rewards the criminal and punishes, not the police, but the innocent victim of the crime and society at large for conduct they may not condone and over which they have little or no control.

Another major failing of the rule is that it has no flexibility, no sense of proportion. It imposes the punishment of evidentiary exclusion for every police misstep, whether malicious or merely mistaken.

In fact, evidence acquired by officers acting with absolute propriety can still be excluded. If an officer

Relying on the exclusionary rule is like curing disease by shooting the patient. Worse, it is like curing A's disease by shooting B. The policeman takes action, apprehends a suspect, and turns him over to the court system. Suppressing evidence months later does not affect him. Instead, by suppressing what is often the best evidence available, it makes prosecution difficult if not impossible.—Carol Corrigan

acts perfectly in accordance with every statute and every case on January 1, but a court decision changes the accepted procedure on February 1, the evidence offered on March 1 will be thrown out, even though everything was done with complete propriety, because the rules were changed long after the game was played. No defendant could be punished in this way; such punishment would constitute an ex post facto application of the law. Yet the courts of this country seek to punish the police, and do actually punish the citizens they serve daily, in just this way, by a retroactive application of the exclusionary rule.

Courts have created an incredibly complex body of Fourth Amendment law. Cases turn on minute factual distinctions, and courts, including the Supreme Court, will frequently disagree on what the requirements actually are. Indeed, judges within the same court often disagree. This intricate, extensive, and ever-changing set of rules must be digested and applied by a police officer, who is not a lawyer, and who must decide in the confusion and danger of the moment if he can detain a suspect, look into his car, or pat-search him for weapons in an attempt to avoid being shot.

The situation has been likened to an inverted pyramid. At the broadest part is the Supreme Court, which often takes months to analyze the problem and even then the justices may not agree. Before the case arrives at that level a court of appeals will have considered it for weeks or months. Before that, lawyers will have spent days or weeks marshalling arguments and writing briefs for preliminary hearing and trial court judges. In the course of this scrutiny, each reviewer looks with calm contemplation over the shoulder of the officer in the field, who, at the point of the pyramid, is expected to make the right decision instantly.

Justice does not bring one's son back, but it is the closest thing to what is right.—a victim's father.

The judicial system purports to be based on the truth. A trial is defined as a search for the truth; and by relying on the truth, it is said, justice will be found. However, the exclusionary rule results in lies. Evidence that has been seized and is highly probative of the defendant's guilt is excluded. From that point on everyone must pretend that it does not exist. The jury is deceived. Facts are ignored or presented misleadingly at judicial direction. The jury is asked to return a just verdict and yet is denied the most telling evidence. It is a delusion to claim that this deception serves justice.

Proponents of the rule claim it protects all citizens, but this assertion is untrue—the exclusionary rule is never an available remedy for the innocent. If the police arrest or search a law-abiding citizen, that citizen has no remedy under the exclusionary rule. By definition, the rule serves only to shield those caught in the commission of a crime or its concealment, because it is only when there is evidence that can be suppressed that the rule comes into play.

Not only does the exclusionary rule benefit the guilty while failing to protect the innocent, the existence and operation of the rule has a disabling effect on the entire justice system. It is sometimes argued that the rule can be tolerated because motions to suppress are granted in only a small proportion of cases. Such an analysis attempts to reveal the size of the iceberg by measuring its tip. However, even when suppression motions are not granted, the provision for them hobbles honest and effective law enforcement at every step and imposes an enormous burden on an already overtaxed system.

Studies relying on the relative infrequency of exclusion fail to take into account any of the following situations created by the exclusionary rule. Cases are not brought to the prosecutor for charging because an officer or his supervisor will realize that the conduct that produced the essential evidence has been barred by a new court decision. If the case is presented, a prosecutor will refuse to file a charge for the same reason. If charges are filed, they may be dismissed or a plea bargain may be entered into rather than take the time and expense to litigate the search issue.

The litigation of these issues is phenomenally costly. The circumstances surrounding the seizure of evidence must be thoroughly investigated by both sides. Extensive witness interviews are conducted. Complete analysis of complex case law is engaged in and often lengthy briefs are filed. Protracted hearings are held during which officers must be taken away from their regular duties or paid overtime for their appearance. The court may take the issue under advisement, often engaging in its own research of the issues. Some rulings can be appealed before the trial is held. If evidence is suppressed, the case is often dismissed or may be so compromised that a plea bargain becomes inevitable. Even if no evidence is suppressed and the defendant is found guilty, search and seizure issues can be raised on post-conviction appeals. Again, appellate lawyers and judges spend vast numbers of hours rebriefing, relitigating, and reevaluating these issues. If the appellate courts reverse the conviction by overturning a search and seizure ruling, the trial of the case must be repeated. Because the appellate process is often time-consuming, such a reversal may mean a case must be retried many years after the crime, when witnesses are no longer available. This delay almost always works to the benefit of the defense. Again, plea bargaining is a frequent result.

The time and effort expended in this process is a major factor in delay and court congestion. Victims are adversely affected by the rule's operation at every turn. When the police fail to solve the crime because of inaction, the victim suffers. When cases are not charged or are dismissed and the "criminal goes free because the constable blundered," [4] the victim is denied justice. When the case is continued interminably or must be retried, the victim is hurt time and time again. The operation of the exclusionary rule is one of the major factors in the public's loss of confidence in the criminal justice system.

I just couldn't believe that the judge could actually suppress this evidence. It's like it really didn't happen . . . it just seems very unfair that something so crucial could be just eliminated.—a victim

The Task Force has concluded that the exclusionary rule does not work, severely compromises the truth-finding process, imposes an intolerable burden on the system, and prevents the court from doing justice. Accordingly, we recommend that the exclusionary rule as it applies to Fourth Amendment issues be abolished.

Alternative methods of deterring police from wrongful actions and methods by which those responsible for the misconduct are held accountable have been suggested. [5] The selection of specific methods is best left to local jurisdictions. However, any of these methods would be more effective in deterring Fourth Amendment violations than the exclusionary rule. They allow for a punishment that is proportionate to the violation. In addition, some are remedies that would be available to all citizens, not just the guilty.

Executive and Legislative Recommendation 6:
Legislation should be proposed and enacted to open parole release hearings to the public.

The requirement that the proceedings of the adult criminal justice system be open to the public has been integral to that system since this nation was founded. Time and again the principle that public scrutiny produces accountability has been reaffirmed. Only the most compelling of reasons can justify the closing of criminal justice proceedings in a free society.

Despite this principle, parole hearings have historically been conducted in secret. Although this was done to protect the parolee, the result has been to insulate parole boards from accountability. Their decisions to release on an unsuspecting public individuals with extensive histories of violence are made in secret. Their reasons for early release are secret. They do not have to justify their conclusions. The public cannot test the validity of their actions or know whether the board is fulfilling its statutory obligation to protect the community.

Every citizen has a vital interest in the proper functioning of the parole board, for its conduct directly affects the safety of the community. Victims of crime hold this general concern even more strongly, for they know from personal experience the danger that the parolee can pose; their safety may be threatened by his release. This Task Force has elsewhere recommended that parole be abolished (see Executive and Legislative Recommendation 7). Until this needed reform is accomplished, however, the parolee's interest in maintaining the current secrecy of parole board proceedings must, on balance, give way to the concern of victims and potential victims for their own safety and the integrity of the system. Opening to public scrutiny the operation of parole boards will go far in helping to restore public confidence in the criminal justice system.

Executive and Legislative Recommendation 7:
Legislation should be proposed and enacted to abolish parole and limit judicial discretion in sentencing.

Victims consistently express anger and frustration with the sentencing and parole systems. As noted ear-

We have truth in advertising and truth in packaging; what is needed is truth in sentencing. Why continue to play this game of giving long sentences that cannot even legally be served?—Thomas Amberg

Our daughter's killer will be eligible for parole when he's 29. For us there is no parole. Our family has been given—with no due process of law—a life sentence of loss and grief.—a victim's parents

lier, victims have a vital and entirely legitimate interest in the sentence that is given to and served by the offender. Their own sense of justice dictates that the person who directly caused them so much agony receive a fair punishment. In addition, they legitimately hope that the offender whom they know is dangerous will be placed where he cannot cause the innocent to suffer.

The interest of victims in seeing their offenders fairly punished and society protected is what enables them to endure the extreme hardships that cooperation with the criminal justice system imposes. When these ends are not accomplished, the victims are justifiably outraged.

When judges have virtually unlimited discretion in imposing sentences, the actual sentence that an offender receives is more a product of the individual philosophy and predilections of the judge than an even-handed analysis of the seriousness of the offense, the harm done the victim, and the history of the offender.

It is equally important that the victim and the community know what the sentence actually means—how long the defendant will be incarcerated. When victims hear the judge impose a life sentence, then meet the offender on the street a few years later because of his release on parole, they lose all faith in the system. The fact is that there is no "truth in sentencing." The system has become so complicated with its various provisions for early release, liberal allowance for "good time," and work and study furloughs, that even practitioners, including judges, have little idea as to when the offender actually will be released.

The system of sentencing that allows for unlimited judicial discretion and parole is deplorable and must be changed. The National Commission on Reform of Federal Criminal Law, the U.S. Department of Justice, the Judiciary Committees of the 93rd through the 96th Congresses, and most recently, the Attorney General's Task Force on Violent Crime, have all strongly expressed dissatisfaction with the current system.

Legislation that abolishes parole and limits judicial discretion in sentencing should be enacted. Legislatures should create sentencing commissions that would establish a set of sentencing guidelines, taking into account variations in types of offenses, the degree of harm caused victims, and the prior convictions and background of the defendant.

With abolition of parole, the sentence imposed would be the sentence served. It should be expected that a prisioner will conform to prison regulations; good time awards should not be required to assist in prison discipline. If some allowances for good time provisions appear to be necessary for maintenance of prison discipline, such allowances should be rigidly controlled; they should be actually earned by the prisoner, not awarded in advance, and should be subject to revocation in the event of prisoner misconduct.

The victim's need for restitution is the same whether or not a period of incarceration is imposed. Therefore, restitution is not obviated by elimination of parole. Court-ordered accountability of the criminal should not end the minute he leaves prison.

If adopted, these provisions would substantially reduce sentencing disparity, establish "truth in sentencing," and meet the needs of victims and society as a whole.

We found real bitterness among victims of crime who later discovered their assailant free after what amounted to a token punishment. I don't think these victims are asking for a pound of flesh. I think they're asking for a measure of justice.—Thomas Amberg

Executive and Legislation Recommendation 8: Legislation should be proposed and enacted to require that school officials report violent offenses against students or teachers, or the possession of weapons or narcotics on school grounds. The knowing failure to make such a report to the police, or deterring others from doing so, should be designated a misdemeanor.

Studies of crime in our nation's schools have shown an intolerably high level of violence directed at both teachers and students;[6] yet relatively few such offenses are reported to police. Many school officials, motivated at least in part by fear of reprisal and by a desire to give the appearance of a safe and well-run institution, minimize or completely deny conduct that occurs there. Problems cannot be solved when they are underestimated or ignored. While these occurrences go unaddressed, students and teachers continue to be assaulted and robbed, and education suffers.

Serious acts of violence and possession of weapons, drugs and other contraband must be reported to the police. To ensure that this is accomplished, school officials should be placed under statutory obligation to report such occurrences, as medical personnel are required to report gunshot wounds or child abuse victims to law enforcement officials. Violation of the duty to report should be made a misdemeanor.

Executive and Legislative Recommendation 9: Legislation should be proposed and enacted to make available to businesses and organizations the sexual assault, child molestation, and pornography arrest records of prospective and present employees whose work will bring them in regular contact with children.

Can't we change the privacy laws so that places of employment can be responsible to those they serve? Here we had a known child molester working with children. Surely we can do better than that.—a victim's mother

Pedophiles and others who prey on children frequently seek employment in or volunteer for positions that give them ready access to youngsters. Although the vast majority who work with the young are dedicated and law-abiding citizens, there are a dangerous few who choose occupations such as recreation director, bus driver, teacher, and coach to have ready access to those they seek to victimize. Many of these individuals have records of violent or exploitative acts against children, but because of privacy laws protecting arrest records, their employers remain ignorant of the danger they impose.

As discussed elsewhere in this report, child molesters have a sexual preference that manifests itself in repeated criminal acts and that is highly resistant to treatment (see Prosecutors Recommendation 8 and Judiciary Recommendation 10). For them, any child might be a potential victim and thus their access to children must be restricted. It is a profound disservice to children to fail to take reasonable and necessary steps for their protection.

A true pedophile, whose sexual preference is the child, is a danger to children all his life, and at least should not be allowed around them.—Irving Prager

Relying on the firmly established and commendable presumption of innocence until guilt is proven, there are laws of privacy that protect arrest records. Difficulty arises, however, in applying this principle to child molestation, in which laws relating to child testimony, institutional disinterest in prosecuting difficult cases, and parental desire to spare children the ordeals of testifying have all combined to produce an abundance of arrests for child molestation, but precious few convictions. As a result, if jurisdictionally permitted, the checking on records of convictions only has failed to adequately safeguard those who need it most: children.

The recommended response to this urgent need by governments is the enactment of legislation that would carve out a narrowly defined exception to laws of privacy by making sexual assault, child molestation and pornography arrest records of prospective and present employees available to businesses and organizations who hire persons whose employment will bring them into regular contact with children.[7]

Executive and Legislative Recommendation 10:
Legislation should be proposed and enacted that would:
  a. Require victim impact statements at sentencing;
  b. Provide for the protection of victims and witnesses from intimidation;
  c. Require restitution in all cases, unless the court provides specific reasons for failing to require it;
  d. Develop and implement guidelines for the fair treatment of crime victims and witnesses; and
  e. Prohibit a criminal from making any profit from the sale of the story of his crime. Any proceeds should be used to provide full restitution to his victims, pay the expenses of his prosecution, and finally, assist the crime victim compensation fund.

Our current system ensures that brokers, and bank tellers are not convicted embezzlers, yet we entrust our children to people operating under the labels of day-care without any sure way of knowing if they have ever been convicted of child molestation. Are our children any less valuable than our money or our other material possessions?—Bea McPherson

Many of the above recommendations have recently been enacted into law on the federal level through the passage of the Omnibus Victims Protection Act of 1982. It is the most comprehensive piece of federal victim legislation to date. Some states have already enacted provisions similar to the Omnibus Victims Protection Act, and those efforts are highly commendable. They are also sources of models for legislation.[8]

The recommended provisions of the Omnibus Victims Protection Act represent a major step in ensuring more humane treatment of victims by a system that is expected to serve them. The recommended provisions provide as follows:

a. The victim impact statement provision requires that the pre-sentence report that is prepared for the judge contain verified information concerning all financial, social, psychological, and medical effects on the crime victim.

b. The protection from intimidation provision expands the definition of who qualifies as a witness in a criminal proceeding and makes any retaliation or intimidation of such a witness illegal. In addition to this statutory protection, however, victims have a strong need for physical security. The Witness Protection Program in the federal government is primarily available to witnesses in organized crime cases; it should be expanded to include innocent victims of violent crime. State and local governments should make a thorough review of the security needs of victims of violent crime in their jurisdictions, and take whatever steps are necessary, including funding provisions, to enable them to meet those needs.

c. The restitution provision requires that the sentencing judge order restitution for property loss and personal injury, unless the court explicitly finds that restitution is not appropriate. This order of restitution can be a condition of probation or parole (see also Judiciary Recommendation 7).

Are we asking too much if we ask to be told when and where the trial will take place? Are we asking too much if we want to be notified of plea bargaining before we read it in the paper?— a victim

d. The guidelines for the fair treatment of crime victims and witnesses seek to mitigate the problems that these citizens encounter in the criminal justice system. The guidelines address nine specific objectives:

(1) The provision of services to victims of crime, including information on compensation for out-of-pocket losses, medical and psychological treatment programs, case status information, and protection from intimidation;

(2) Prompt notification to victims and witnesses of scheduling changes in court proceedings;

(3) Prompt notification to victims of violent crime concerning their cases, including the arrest and bond status of the defendant, and the eventual outcome of the case;

(4) Consultation with the victim during the various stages of the prosecution;

(5) Separate waiting areas for defense and prosecution witnesses awaiting court proceedings;

(6) Prompt return of property seized as evidence or recovered during an investigation;

(7) Contacting a victim's employer and creditors to seek their cooperation, by explaining the situation of the victim after the crime, the necessity of

court appearances, and his temporary inability to meet outstanding debts (see also Private Sector Recommendations 1 and 3);

(8) Training law enforcement personnel in victim assistance; and

(9) The provision of general victim assistance in a variety of areas, such as transportation, parking, and translators.

e. The provision prohibiting a felon from profiting from the sale of the story of his crime ensures that no felon profits financially as the result of publicity resulting from his criminal conduct.

Executive and Legislative Recommendation 11:
Legislation should be proposed and enacted to establish or expand employee assistance programs for victims of crime employed by the government.

Victims of crime and the problems that they face are so numerous that it requires the coordinated effort of many organizations and individuals, in both the government and the private sector, to help them recover from the crime and contribute to a successful prosecution (see Private Sector Recommendation 2). Even an excellently staffed and operated victim/witness assistance unit depends on the cooperation and good will of other sources. Employee assistance programs are an excellent resource.

Agencies in the federal government are mandated to establish and operate employee assistance programs.[9] These programs were established to assist employees whose job performance has been jeopardized by mental health problems or drug or alcohol abuse. The psychological trauma that violent crime produces can frequently affect work performance. A comprehensive program to assist victims of crime benefits both the employee and the government. Government will ultimately benefit by improved job performance.

Examination of jurisdictions that have victim/witness assistance units has shown that many victims are unaware of the existence of such units. An individual is more likely to be aware of a service provided through his employment than he is of a unit associated with the criminal justice system.

Employee assistance programs can perform many services. Trained counselors can both advise the em-

Shouldn't we be notified if the killer is out on bond, or if he is about to come up for a parole hearing? Had my son lived through the assault on him, would he not be entitled to this information? He didn't live through this, and I think that I am entitled to ask it for him and for all the victims who don't survive.—a victim's mother

When one has been brutally attacked and injured, even a friendly and understanding voice on the phone can help overcome some of the sense of physical and psychological helplessness brought on by being a victim.—a victim

When the police were notified, they immediately took my daughter to the hospital for examination and treatment. But to add insult to injury, we were required to pay nearly $200 for the rape kit and emergency room treatment.—a victim's mother

ployee and explain his situation to his supervisor. They can maintain a list of mental health practitioners qualified to assist victims. They can help the victim with any difficulties that arise with creditors, and can refer them to needed social service and victim compensation programs. The existence of such a program conveys to the employee that his employer is concerned about his welfare and supports his willingness to assist the criminal justice system.

A number of states have also set up programs for their employees. The beneficial aspects of governmental programs are twofold: first, their employees receive direct assistance at the workplace, and second, they serve as a role model for organizations in the private sector. Federal, state, and local governments should fully support and expand employee assistance programs, with additional emphasis on assisting victims of crime.

Executive and Legislative Recommendation 12: Legislation should be proposed and enacted to ensure that sexual assault victims are not required to assume the cost of physical examinations and materials used to obtain evidence.

A primary purpose of the physical examination of rape victims by doctors and emergency room personnel is the collection of evidence. Effective prosecution may be impossible without the results of a timely examination of the victim.

Although the physical exam is essentially an investigative process, rape victims are routinely required to pay for the examination themselves. Victims of other crimes, such as burglary or robbery, are not charged when the police examine their homes for latent fingerprints and it is unfair and inappropriate to assess rape victims for the cost of evidence collection.

To rectify this injustice, the budget of police departments, prosecutors' offices, or public hospitals should be increased to cover the cost of physical examinations and materials used to obtain evidence from rape victims. These funds would not cover the cost of any additional medical treatment that the victim requires as a result of physical injuries. These latter costs are best covered by victim compensation (see Federal Executive and Legislative Recommendation 1).

Proposed Federal Action

The foregoing recommendations of this Task Force are meant for consideration at both the federal and state levels. Those that follow are concerned specifically with efforts most properly undertaken by the federal government; they include recommendations for Congressionally directed funding of certain types of programs and of selected areas for further study.

Recommendations

1. Congress should enact legislation to provide federal funding to assist state crime victim compensation programs.

2. Congress should enact legislation to provide federal funding, reasonably matched by local revenues, to assist in the operation of federal, state, local, and private nonprofit victim/witness assistance agencies that make comprehensive assistance available to all victims of crime.

3. The federal government should establish a federally based resource center for victim and witness assistance.

4. The President should establish a task force to study the serious problem of violence within the family, including violence against children, spouse abuse, and abuse of the elderly, and to review and evaluate national, state, and local efforts to address this problem.

5. A study should be commissioned at the federal level to evaluate the juvenile justice system from the perspective of the victim.

6. The Task Force endorses the principle of accountability for gross negligence of parole board officials in releasing into the community dangerous criminals who then injure others. A study should be commissioned at the federal level to determine how, and under what circumstances, this principle of accountability should be implemented.

Commentary

Federal Executive and Legislative Recommendation 1:
Congress should enact legislation to provide federal funding to assist state crime victim compensation programs.

38

This Task Force believes that financial compensation for losses that victims sustain as a result of violent crime must be an integral part of both federal and state governments' response to assisting these innocent citizens. No amount of money can erase the tragedy and trauma imposed on them; however, some financial redress can be an important first step in helping people begin the often lengthy process of recovery. For some, this modest financial assistance can be the lifeline that preserves not only some modicum of stability and dignity but also life itself. As indicated elsewhere in this report, the financial and nonfinancial losses that victims suffer are severalfold: exorbitant and unanticipated medical costs, lost wages, altered careers, and prolonged psychological trauma.

The financial impact of crime can be severe. There is a tendency to believe that insurance will cover most costs and losses. While some victims are made whole through adequate coverage, many others are not. The poor and the elderly often have no insurance. Even those victims who have coverage discover that recovery is made difficult or impossible by high deductible clauses, problems with market value assessment for unique items, and limited or precluded payment for such expenses as lost wages and psychological counseling.

Ordering the offender to pay restitution is a laudable goal that should be actively pursued, but its limitations must be recognized. A restitution order cannot even be made unless the criminal is caught and successfully prosecuted. Even when such an order is imposed, it does not help the victim if the defendant is without resources or if the ordering court does not enforce its order. In addition, even if complete restitution is made, it may take years to be accomplished. In the interim, the victim is left to bear the cost as well as he is able.

The problem is not just one of payment; it may be an issue of feeding the family or not losing the house while waiting for payment to be made. A victim compensation fund has an obvious function in such cases. Certainly, if monies are eventually recovered from insurance or restitution payments, such amounts can be repaid into the compensation fund. This Task Force examined the efficacy of some existing state compensation funds and has developed suggestions for federal participation.

State Compensation Programs

Thirty-six states and the District of Columbia now have crime victim compensation programs.[10] The philosophical basis for these programs varies from a legal tort theory, whereby the state is seen to have failed to protect its citizens adequately, to a humanitarian rationale through which all citizens should receive assistance for their compelling needs, to a by-products theory that recognizes victim satisfaction as a benefit to the criminal justice system. In reality, most programs represent a mixture of these rationales.

Whatever the basis for their adoption, state programs now share a common concern, the acquisition of adequate funding.[11] In many states, program availability is not advertised for fear of depleting available resources or overtaxing a numerically inadequate staff. Victim claims may have to wait months until sufficient fines have been collected or until a new fiscal year begins and the budgetary fund is replenished. Creditors are seldom patient. While waiting for funding that will eventually come, victims can be sued civilly, harassed continually, or forced to watch their credit rating vanish. Not only is compensation important, its payment also must be timely to save victims inconvenience, embarrassment and substantial, long-term financial hardship.

The availability of unencumbered emergency assistance is also critical to many victims of violence. Immediate needs for food, shelter, and medical assistance cannot be deferred for the weeks or months it may take to process paper work. While many states provide emergency funds in theory, their failure to adequately fund these programs means that little actual relief is available in practice. Not many programs have been able to generate true emergency assistance where needed.[12] It is cold comfort to a hungry or homeless victim to learn that his state had thought about helping him but, unfortunately, emergency funds ran out three months ago.

Funding constraints also discourage programs from eliminating or raising the maximum allowable award.

In order to apply, a victim virtually needs an attorney. The process is still then quite lengthy and provides no immediate assistance for the victim whose children are hungry or whose gas has been disconnected because her money was stolen and she had no way to pay her bill.—Fern Ferguson

Available data suggest, however, that the number of claims approaching the maximum are few.[13] A blanket maximum can severely disadvantage those most needy and worthy of assistance. One example is that of a young man who had just finished college and had no medical insurance when he became the victim of a brutal assault. Now in a body cast and blind in one eye, he has amassed medical bills of $30,000. He still needs extensive treatment and therapy. The maximum compensation award in his state is $10,000. At the age of 22 he is permanently disabled, may have to forego medical care he needs but cannot afford, and faces debts that it may take a lifetime to repay.[14]

Whether the compensation funds come from general revenues, fines and penalties, or a combination of these, states should aggressively track their own progress in meeting victim needs. If the number of eligible applications is increasing, legislatures should be prepared to increase fund contributions accordingly. When offender fines are not being adequately collected, steps must be taken to identify problem areas and take appropriate action. Noncollection may stem from judicial apathy, local hesitancy to divert money to state coffers, or the inefficiency or disinterest of prosecutors and probation officers. At least one state employs a full-time court monitor to audit court records and verify that appropriate fine revenues are being submitted to the victim compensation program.[15] Furthermore, states should periodically examine the administrative burden that has developed around the evaluation of claims to ensure that administrative costs do not divert a disproportionate share of the budget away from the meeting of victim needs.

Finally, some states are now using additional revenue sources for compensation funds, particularly since the level of available general revenues is shrinking. In some states a compensation award is made, and if the victim later receives restitution payments from the offender, the payments are returned to the compensation fund. Several states divert to the fund a small percentage of the salaries earned by offenders on work release or in prison.[16] Other states have ordered that a defendant's profits from the sale of books or films based on his criminal activity must go to the compensation fund. Still other states provide that bail bond forfeitures be paid into the fund. Some of these new funding mechanisms have yet to prove their effectiveness; however, it behooves compensation programs to explore a multiplicity of funding sources, as many victim services programs have done, to improve their ability to provide assistance.

Funding problems are the most dramatic and the most visible for compensation programs because their survival is contingent on solving them. At the same time, economics should not overshadow other less pervasive but nonetheless important issues with which state programs must come to grips. The testimony of both crime victims and experts appearing before the Task Force points to several other areas that warrant particular attention.

Those who administer compensation programs must remember that they are working in an area of government service to citizens whose lives have been altered by tragedy and subjected to hardship. One woman who suffered extensive nerve damage when she was forced to fall to the floor at gunpoint by an armed robber saw her life and that of her family drastically changed. Medical bills and the loss of a job that she was no longer physically able to perform created a desperate financial situation. When she first applied for compensation, she was inaccurately told that her claim was disqualified as untimely. When she reapplied, she received a form letter reading: "It is not clear whether you can be considered a victim of a violent crime . . . as you were never physically touched by any of the suspects." [17]

Another issue is whether victims who are related to, or are living with, the offender should be excluded from payment eligibility. The states' desire to minimize fraud is laudable; however, many innocent victims of violence in the home are being unfairly ignored. Some states have successfully experimented with allowing flexibility in this area as long as the award will not unjustly benefit the offender. A blanket exclusion can be particularly devastating to child victims of intra-family abuse who, as a result, are denied adequate treatment.

Crime victims and those who serve them repeatedly voiced concern over minimum loss requirements enacted by legislatures to contain costs. In practice, this exclusion places the elderly and low-income victims at a distinct disadvantage; a threshold of $100 or $250 represents to them a substantial loss that they cannot absorb. These limits also prevent rape victims from receiving compensation for the cost of rape examination and evidence collection procedures (see Executive and Legislative Recommendation 12). States are beginning to exclude elderly and fixed-income victims from these requirements and some are considering the exclusion of rape victims as well.[18]

Similarly, most programs will not compensate for property losses—although for the elderly, for example, the loss of a television set or a hearing aid may result in the loss of contact with the outside world. Victim services directors testified repeatedly that greater flexibility is needed. Rather than attempting to list the classes of victims or kinds of expenses exempted from minimum or property loss requirements, the better practice seems to be the drafting of legislation allowing compensation for "other reasonable expenses" as may be determined by the administrator of the fund.

Finally, programs differ greatly in their residency requirements. Some states will only compensate residents who are victimized within their boundaries. Others will compensate their residents regardless of where they are victimized but will not compensate nonresidents who are victimized within the state. States that attract large numbers of tourists have been hesitant to offer coverage to nonresidents for fear of depleting the compensation fund. One man interviewed by the Task Force, a resident of state A, had been brutally stabbed while vacationing in state B. He was told that state A would compensate him only if he had been stabbed at home, while state B would not compensate out-of-state residents. Though he was no less a victim, there was no provision for his compensation.

At least 15 states have entered into reciprocal agreements. Although this policy is a first step toward an equitable approach, it is limited. To address the problem fully, states should agree either to compensate all eligible individuals victimized within a state, regardless of residency, or to compensate their own residents wherever they are victimized.

The Task Force's inquiry has shown that substantial progress has been made by many states in their attempts to compensate crime victims. The Task Force commends these states for their pioneering efforts to begin to meet victims' needs. However, the states' inability to fully address the problems that persist suggest that there is an important role for the federal government to play in this area.

Federal Involvement

Any discussion of federal funding for victim compensation revolves around two issues: propriety of federal involvement and cost. There are at least two sound bases for federal participation in victim compensation. First, most state programs currently compensate federal crime victims; however, because of the financial exigencies outlined above, they may be unwilling or unable to continue doing so. If state programs stop helping victims of federal crimes and no federal efforts are made, then either there would be no help available for such victims, or victims of crimes over which federal and state governments share jurisdiction would find that their eligibility for assistance depends on a bureaucratic decision as to which jurisdiction will prosecute. These decisions are based on considerations that have nothing whatever to do with the condition of the victim. Furthermore, such a victim would be in a state of perpetual limbo if no one was apprehended for the crime and thus no charging decision was ever made.

At the time of my husband's murder, I was about seven months pregnant. When my husband died, we were totally without income to purchase the bare necessities. Eventually social security assisted me, but that was not for nearly five months when I had a small infant at home.—a victim's wife

The federal government could, of course, commit itself to aiding victims of federal crimes. If this course is chosen, a new bureaucracy covering 50 states would have to be created. The start-up and continued administrative costs would be substantial. The duplication of state and federal effort would not only be inefficient but also would be confusing to the victims both entities seek to serve. The most unfortunate result of this course would be that large sums would be expended unnecessarily on administration rather than made available to those victims who need assistance.

Second, the federal government has made substantial sums of money available to states for state prisons as well as for the education and rehabilitation of state prisoners who have committed state crimes. If the federal government will step in to assist state prisoners, it seems only just that the same federal government not shrink from aiding the innocent taxpaying citizens victimized by those very prisoners the government is assisting.

It should also be noted that, beyond the compensation issue, the federal government, like local governments, needs victim/witness programs to assist those who become involved with federal prosecutions. The distinction between these two areas should be clear. Victim compensation boards currently operate at the state level and make money available to reimburse victims for out-of-pocket costs they incur as a result of medical bills, therapy costs, funeral expenses, etc. Victim/witness assistance programs operate at the municipal or county level and help victims in a number of ways, including explaining the justice system, accompanying them to court, arranging transportation, interceding with creditors, referring them to counselors, and assisting them in applying for victim compensation and emergency services.

It is possible to address the issue of costs in such a way that imprecise figures need not be relied upon and the potential for cost overruns is eliminated. The Task Force suggests that a Crime Victim's Assistance Fund be created and that it rely in part on federal criminal fines, penalties, and forfeitures that currently are paid directly into the general fund. Not only is it appropriate that these monies collected as a result of criminal activity be used to help victims, but this method of funding also ensures a program that is both administratively efficient and self-sufficient, requiring no funding from tax revenues.

It is proposed that the fund be administered in the following fashion. The first step is the acquisition of monies. There are six measures that can be relied upon to produce revenues. First, the Task Force endorses the recommendation proposed by the Criminal Code Revision that fines and penalties for violations of Title 18 and Title 21 of the United States Code be doubled or tripled. Second, in those cases in which the criminal realizes a gain or the victim suffers a loss that exceeds the maximum fine, the judge should be empowered to impose a fine that is double the gain or loss. Many federal crimes result in tremendous losses to victims and gains to criminals. If the criminal knows he can realize an enormous benefit while risking only a fine that represents a miniscule fraction of what he may acquire, there is no incentive for him to refrain from committing the crime. Not only will such provision result in penalties that are more appropriate to the crime, but they will also substantially increase the monies available to the fund. Third, efforts by the U.S. Department of Justice should be intensified to improve current fine collection and accounting procedures. Fourth, the fund should be augmented by a fee assessed in addition to any fine or other penalty on all those convicted of federal offenses. The fee would be paid at the time of sentencing and would range from $10 to $100 for misdemeanants and from $25 to $500 for felons. Fifth, a percentage of all federal forfeitures should be earmarked for the fund. Sixth, revenues collected through the excise tax on the sale of handguns could be diverted into the fund. This tax money currently is placed in the Pittman-Robertson Fund, which supports the maintenance of hunting preserves, certain wildlife studies, and a hunter education program. When initiated in 1937, the Pittman-Robertson Fund was supported solely by taxes on the sale of hunting rifles; the fund today continues to inure primarily to the benefit of hunting enthusiasts. In 1970, new legislation added the revenues from handgun taxes to the fund. There is little if any relation between handguns and hunting or wildlife activity. There is a substantial relationship, however, between handguns and the commission of violent crime. It should be noted that the diversion of these monies into the Crime Victim's Assistance Fund will only reduce the Pittman-Robertson Fund by about 25 percent of its total every year. The Task Force suggests that Congress reevaluate its priorities with regard to the use of these funds. It appears that the implementation of this suggestion will not unduly impede the contribution made to hunters and wildlife protection by the Pittman-Robertson Fund, will substantially assist victims whose pressing needs are not now being met, and will direct the proceeds of this tax to a goal more closely related to the items that give rise to the revenue.

Once the monies have been acquired, the fund will be divided in two equal parts. The first half of the fund would be designated the Federal Victim Compensation Fund, monies from which will be disbursed to existing state compensation programs that meet the guidelines set out below. The decision to give money

*I called Social
Services after the
molestations and I
felt that they were
more interested in the
defendants than in
my daughter. They
advised the
defendants to get into
voluntary treatment
because it would go
better for them in
court. This counseling
was paid for by us,
the taxpayers. Social
Services told me
where I could find
treatment for my
daughter, but they
also said that I would
have to pay for it.—a
victim's mother*

to existing programs rather than to provide seed money for new programs rests on two bases. Programs already in existence are currently giving service and need financial help; they are currently meeting the needs of victims and should not be disadvantaged. Further, requiring that local government assume the initial cost of starting the program and the primary responsibility for continued funding assures the existence of a genuine local commitment rather than the initiation of a proposal simply to put a claim in for available federal funds. No state program should be eligible for a portion of the compensation fund unless it provides compensation for anyone victimized within its borders, regardless of the victim's state of residency; provides compensation regardless of whether the crime violates state or federal law; and provides compensation for psychological counseling required as a result of victimization.

Monies from the compensation fund would be awarded among the states as follows: all states would report the total amount of compensation awarded in the previous year, and those figures would be totaled to give the total compensation awarded nationally. Each state's award would be figured in terms of its percentage of the national total. Each state would be awarded that percentage of the compensation fund for the ensuing year with the limitation that it could not receive more than 10 percent of its total awards for the previous year. The 10 percent limitation will guard against depletion of the compensation fund and against larger states drawing off too large a segment of the fund. Any monies not dispersed would shift to the Federal Victim/Witness Assistance Fund.

The second half of the Crime Victim's Assistance Fund would be denoted the Federal Victim/Witness Assistance Fund; the monies allotted thereto would be used to support victim/witness assistance programs throughout the federal, state, and local system. (This proposal is discussed more fully in Federal Executive and Legislative Recommendation 2.)

The Task Force suggests that a sunset clause be added to the legislation proposed above whereby, in three years, the Attorney General would be required to reevaluate the effectiveness of this legislation and report to Congress as to whether it is the most efficient, effective, and fair way for the government to assist state compensation and victim/witness assistance programs. If, at the end of four years, Congress has not taken action on the Attorney General's report, this legislation would cease to remain in effect.

Federal Executive and Legislative Recommendation 2: Congress should enact legislation to provide federal funding, reasonably matched by local revenues, to assist in the operation of federal, state, local, and private nonprofit victim/witness agencies that make comprehensive assistance available to all victims of crime.

A unit composed solely of persons dedicated to helping both victims and witnesses is essential to meeting their needs (see Appendix 2). The efforts of those individuals, often provided on a volunteer basis, shine brightly in the otherwise dim landscape of general institutional neglect of those on whom the criminal justice system relies.

In spite of their good record of performance, victim/witness assistance units have recently encountered serious financial difficulties as governments across the nation have been forced to make budget cuts. Some units have ceased functioning; others have had to seriously curtail their services because of reductions in staff and operating funds.

From a fiscal standpoint, it is indeed unfortunate that the very existence of victim/witness assistance units is in doubt in many jurisdictions. A well-run unit can be extremely cost effective. It is expensive to arrest someone and prosecute him in court. When the case is dismissed because the witnesses were not notified or failed to appear out of frustration with the criminal justice system, that money is simply wasted. Meanwhile, the freed defendant may commit more crimes. In addition, victim/witness assistance units that use an effective on-call system can produce substantial savings in witness fees and police overtime pay.[19]

Composed of people who are dedicated to helping victims, many units have done all they can to continue services on reduced budgets. It is clear, however, that they need additional revenues to continue their operation and expand their services as recommended elsewhere in this report. The view of the

At the preliminary hearing I finally was put in contact with the victim/witness staff and their help has been tremendous. I only wish it had come sooner.—a victim

Waiting for the compensation to clear was very difficult. The hospital was very concerned about the payment of the bills; I even had a civil action filed against me. The victim/witness coordinator went into court with me, helped me to file some responses, and helped to get the hospital to wait for the funds to be approved.—a victim

*I was put in touch
with a woman in the
victim/witness unit
who had recently lost
a daughter in a
brutal homicide. She
talked with me, got
me out of my shell,
and gave me
strength.—a victim*

*Even though the
person who brutally
beat my husband was
never caught, and we
wish he had been, the
help we received from
the victim/witness
unit was essential to
my husband's
recovery and our
survival.—a victim*

*If I have learned
anything that this
Task Force should
understand, it is that
there is a need for
some kind of victim
assistance programs
that reach out and
seek to help people
who are too
emotionally involved
in cases to seek help
themselves.—a victim*

Task Force is that although the federal government should not fully subsidize such units, their praiseworthy efforts must be encouraged, both by assisting units already in existence and by providing incentives for the initiation of new programs. There are many jurisdictions in this country in which victims of violent crime receive little or no help. This failure to assist those whom the system exists to serve and on whom it depends is unacceptable.

This Task Force does not make lightly a recommendation that the federal government expend funds for what is primarily a state and local responsibility. In this case, however, the need is great and the benefits are evident; furthermore, a failure to recognize both the federal obligation and the federal interest to be served could result in a serious disservice to honest citizens who seek nothing more than fair and courteous treatment from their government.

Accordingly, this Task Force recommends that the second half of the Federal Crime Victims Assistance Fund be designated the Federal Victim/Witness Assistance Fund (see Federal Executive and Legislative Recommendation 1), and that monies from that fund be made available to state and local victim/witness assistance units. Consistent with the view that the location of the unit is best left to local determination, the funds should be dispersed to units whether they are established within the criminal justice system or in the private sector, including units operating in hospitals. High priority should be given to units that utilize community volunteers and receive other support from the private sector.

Most U.S. Attorneys' Offices have not yet established victim/witness assistance units.[20] The federal government should provide a role model for other jurisdictions. It is essential that federal victims' and witnesses' needs be met. Because the majority of violent crime is prosecuted at the state level, federal prosecutors deal with proportionately fewer civilian victims and witnesses. Accordingly, we recommend that 20 percent of the Federal Victim/Witness Assistance Fund be reserved to assist federal victims and witnesses, with the balance made available to the states.

Federal Executive and Legislative Recommendation 3:
The federal government should establish a federally
based resource center for victim and witness assistance.

This proposed resource center would serve as a national clearinghouse of information concerning victim and witness assistance programs, victim compensation programs, and organizations from the private sector that seek to assist victims and witnesses. It should establish liaison with national, state, local, and private sector organizations whose activities are directed toward improved services for victims and witnesses. It should monitor the status of compensation programs and victim/witness legislation. In addition, the center should maintain a directory of state, local, and private sector programs and experts in the field to facilitate communication and the transfer of expertise.

This center is essential because the sources of information in this area are many, and they are found at all levels in the public and private sector. In addition, these sources are located throughout the country. With increased attention in this area, many different groups need information to augment or implement programs to help victims. Because resources are precious, it is essential that these new and existing groups benefit from the work that has preceded them as well as from new insights acquired through the successful provision of services.

Federal Executive and Legislative Recommendation 4:
The President should establish a Task Force to study
the serious problem of violence within the family,
including violence against children, spouse abuse, and
abuse of the elderly, and to review and evaluate
national, state, and local efforts to address this
problem.

Family violence is often much more complex in both its causes and its solutions than nonfamily violence. Violence within a home can be directed at children, at spouses, or at elderly family members, and for those who live in a home where violence occurs, the pressures are tremendous. The assaults affect everyone in the house, not only the immediate victim, because of the ever-present quality of the threat of violence.

The decision to report this type of conduct to authorities is agonizing. The victim wrestles with feelings of fear, loyalty, love, guilt, and shame; often there is a sense of responsibility for other victims in the household. The victim also knows that reporting is a risk. All too often police or prosecutors minimize or ignore the problem and the victim is left alone to face an attacker who will respond with anger at being reported or incarcerated.

Because of the differences in the causes, manifestations, and effects of family violence, the system must be flexible in its response. Unlike the victims of other crimes, family violence victims often do not want their attacker punished; they simply want the violence to stop. Especially, in those cases in which violence is episodic or alcohol-related, the victim wishes to preserve the more positive aspects of family life. Putting the attacker in jail can also punish the victim and others in the family when a job is lost or bail money and fines are taken from the family budget. In addition, incarceration does not resolve the underlying problems that lead to violence and may only exacerbate the situation upon the assailant's release. However, when the pattern of violence has been long-standing or the injuries severe, conventional prosecution is called for.

It is the strong sense of this Task Force that the cries of family violence victims can no longer go unheeded. Because of the complexities of the problem and the significant ways in which the phenomenon differs from crime imposed by those outside the family, it was impossible for this Task Force to address this issue in the manner and depth it requires. Accordingly, we recommend that a new Presidential task force thoroughly study the problem of family violence, paying particular attention to the integration of government and other community resources to assist these victims.

**Federal Executive and Legislative Recommendation 5:
A study should be commissioned at the federal level to
evaluate the juvenile justice system from the
perspective of the victim.**

The criminal justice system is disturbingly inconsistent
in the way it treats juvenile victims and juvenile victimizers. This divergence exists, in part, because society has developed two independent systems based on
widely divergent presuppositions. If a child is a
victim, that child is expected to come to an adult
court, open to the public, and behave like an adult,
speak like an adult, comprehend like an adult, and
meet adult standards. The motivation underlying this
treatment is the protection of adult suspects against
the testimony of children, who are considered less
trustworthy or accurate than adults.

The juvenile justice system, on the other hand,
begins with the premise that those who have not
reached adulthood cannot be truly held accountable
for their actions; they do not intend to do harm and
will reform if shown the error of their ways. As a
result, in many jurisdictions even violent and frequent
dangerous conduct is not considered criminal, and is
evaluated behind closed doors. Society is paying a
tremendous price for this system. The Task Force
suggests that the different treatment of juvenile victims and juvenile victimizers be carefully reevaluated.

Those who undertake the study of the juvenile justice system should be charged to consider the needs
of the innocent victims and the society as a whole.
Too often in the past, analyses of this area have fo-
cused solely on the benefits to be extended to offenders while ignoring the needs of a society burdened by
their offenses. The existing inequities and the policies
that contribute to them should be closely examined.

There will always be instances in which youngsters,
because of a youthful tendency to excess or a lack of
experience and insight, commit acts that are more
harmful than they anticipated or intended. The existing juvenile justice system was established, basically,
to address these kinds of offenses. However, many juvenile offenses drastically exceed this type of conduct.
Armed robbery, rape, and murder cannot be laid at
the door of mere immaturity or youthful exuberance.
The victims of these crimes are no less traumatized
because the offender was under age. A substantial

*Child victims of crime
are specially
handicapped. First,
the criminal justice
system distrusts them,
and puts special
barriers in their path of
prosecuting their
claims to justice.
Second, the criminal
justice system seems
indifferent to the
legitimate special
needs that arise from
their participation. —
David Lloyd*

proportion of the violent crime in this country is committed by juveniles, who are becoming more violent at an increasingly early age. Both the reasons and suitable correctives for this are unknown. Are there rational corrections for these offenders that provide a deterrent? Is there a decline in the teaching of moral values in schools and the home that serves as a contributing factor? Does violence in television programs and movies and ready access to pornography exacerbate the problem?

The Task Force is cognizant of many studies in the juvenile area; none, however, focuses on the accountability and the responsibility of the juvenile criminal to his victim.

Juveniles too often are not held accountable for their conduct, and the system perpetuates this lack of accountability. When juveniles cause financial harm they are seldom required to make restitution. If they or their parents cannot or will not pay for reimbursement of the victim, often none is made. Thus, the juvenile is not required to face the consequences of his behavior; others—his parents or the victim—must bear the consequences for him.

The judge found him guilty in juvenile court of shooting my son in the back and killing him and sentenced him to 5 years in the detention center. He'll only do one and a half years and then he'll be free. For killing my son he only does one and a half years!—a victim's mother

The subject of juvenile punishment as a whole should be reexamined. It is unacceptable for a juvenile who commits murder to serve only a year in custody. Imposing such a sentence implies to both the killer and the victim's family that expiation for the life taken can be accomplished in 12 months. It must be faced that some juvenile offenders are more sophisticated about crime, the way in which the system operates, and how they can avoid being held culpable than are many adults. The method of punishment for those juveniles who have documented criminal histories or who have committed serious violent crimes should be critically reevaluated. The current policies of many jurisdictions neither reform nor punish; they only teach juveniles that they can act with relative impunity if they learn how to take advantage of the system. Ways to deal effectively with the juvenile who has graduated to committing adult violent offenses must be devised.

The Task Force suggests that the juvenile justice system be modified to provide that youths, 15 years of age or older, who commit murder, rape, armed robbery, armed burglary, or assault with the intent to commit these crimes be tried as an adult. These are adult crimes and those who commit them should be held accountable as adults. Under such a modification, the prosecutor would retain the option of bringing charges against such an offender in the existing juvenile system. The Task Force is of the opinion that existing waiver provisions have been inadequate and recommends reserving this option to the prosecutor, leaving open the possibility of juvenile treatment if the particular circumstances of the case warrant such treatment.

After sentencing, no individual tried as an adult should be placed in a juvenile facility. In some jurisdictions, defendants who are over the statutory age for treatment as juveniles and who are convicted in adult courts may still be sentenced to juvenile facilities. In many instances, the adult sentence imposed can be modified by youth authorities with the result that an armed robber may serve only a few months in custody, rather than the term of years prescribed in the sentence. Further, the placement in such facilities of those 15 years of age and older who commit violent crimes makes those institutions far more dangerous for the nonviolent juveniles who are appropriately being housed there.

Policies supporting the sealing of juvenile records should be studied. The theory that an individual should not be disadvantaged for life because of an isolated mistake as a youngster is one that has merit. The premise supporting such a policy is that the juvenile crime is a not very serious aberration in an otherwise responsible life. The juvenile who commits serious offenses presents a different case entirely. If such a person continues to commit crimes as an adult, serious consideration should be given to allowing the admission of his juvenile record at adult trials and sentencing hearings. The sealing of records should be a safeguard for those who correct their conduct; it should not be a screen behind which the demonstrably dangerous can hide.

The issue of safety in the schools should also be addressed. Students should enjoy the right to go to school without the risk of being stabbed, robbed, approached by drug dealers, or harmed by persons under the influence of drugs. School administrators must regain the capacity for supervision that is necessary to restore safety to the environment in which children spend so many hours daily.

Federal Executive and Legislative Recommendation 6: The Task Force endorses the principle of accountability for gross negligence of parole board officials in releasing into the community dangerous criminals who then injure others. A study should be commissioned at the federal level to determine how, and under what circumstances, this principle of accountability should be implemented.

The Parole Board that let him out did an awful, ignorant, foolish thing. They just turned their back on society, they just didn't care about the public. They knew about him and what he might do and they let him out anyway.— a victim

Every day, individuals with long records of violence are released from prisons on parole. Although parole boards are generally required to consider the degree of danger that a prospective parolee represents before ordering his return to the community, there are many cases in which obviously dangerous prisoners are precipitously released. These criminals are then free to commit new crimes. The innocent victims of these crimes, and their families, soon learn that parole boards operate in secrecy and are not accountable to anyone for their decisions.

Because of this lack of accountability and many other problems identified by this Task Force, we have recommended that the current parole system be abolished (see Executive and Legislative Recommendation 7). Until such abolition takes place, this Task Force endorses the principle that parole board officials should be held accountable for acts of gross negligence.

A number of methods have been proposed for implementing this principle. One of those allows suits against the government by persons or their families who are injured by obviously dangerous parolees who have been released through gross negligence. A number of lawsuits have already attempted to utilize this relatively new theory of liability, with varying results.[21] The principal barrier to this litigation has been that the doctrine of sovereign immunity has not been waived in actions challenging "discretionary functions" of government officials.[22] It has been proposed that sovereign immunity be restricted to allow for challenging the discretionary decisions of parole boards if they are grossly negligent. However, important questions remain; the fiscal effect of such action is not clear, nor is the likelihood that such action will deter future gross negligence by parole officials. Also uncertain is how the Federal Tort Claims Act or similar state provisions should be amended to permit such suits.

Another way to hold parole boards accountable is to create an effective method of disciplinary action for parole board members. Although this method does not offer any financial assistance to injured victims, it should serve as an effective deterrent to grossly negligent releases, and therefore obviate the need for financial assistance to victims of violent parolees. Whether the deterrent effect will be sufficient to accomplish this goal is open to debate.

A thorough study of these and other possible implementation strategies should be undertaken. Careful consideration should be given to the questions raised above as well as any other related issues.

Proposed Action for Criminal Justice System Agencies

The actions of certain elements of the criminal justice system—the police, prosecutors, the judiciary, and parole boards—are guided not only by law but also by rules, regulations, and procedural codes. The following recommendations of this Task Force are proposals for change at this level.

Recommendations for Police

The police are often the first on the scene; it is to them, the first source of protection, that the victim first turns. They should be mindful that, in fulfilling their obligation to solve the crime and apprehend the criminal, they must also treat victims with the attention due them. The manner in which police officers treat a victim affects not only his immediate and long-term ability to deal with the event but also his willingness to assist in a prosecution. The foundation of all interactions between police and victims should be the knowledge that it is these citizens whom the officer has sworn the serve. These recommendations are meant to ensure better treatment of victims by police.

1. Police departments should develop and implement training programs to ensure that police officers are:
   a. Sensitive to the needs of victims; and
   b. Informed, knowledgeable, and supportive of the existing local services and programs for victims.
2. Police departments should establish procedures for the prompt photographing and return of property to victims (with the prosecutor's approval).
3. Police departments should establish procedures to ensure that victims of violent crime are periodically informed of the status and closing of investigations.
4. Police officers should give a high priority to investigating witnesses' reports of threats or intimidation and should forward these reports to the prosecutor.

Commentary

Police Recommendation 1:

Police departments should develop and implement training programs to ensure that police officers are:
   a. Sensitive to the needs of victims; and
   b. Informed, knowledgeable, and supportive of the existing local services and programs for victims.

The arresting officer was wonderful—he made all the difference in the world.—a victim

After I managed to loosen the ropes with which I was tied up, I went to my neighbor's and immediately called for the police. They didn't arrive for more than an hour, and when they did arrive, they were very rude and insensitive. Despite my bruises and my excited condition, the first police officer who arrived, asked me "Lady, what makes you think you were raped?"—a victim

The Task Force wishes to note that many victims spoke very highly of the officers with whom they had contact. As a group, policemen were the most warmly praised of any professionals in the system. Unfortunately, however, some victims were treated in a manner that was insensitive, uncaring, and even hostile. Training can help eliminate this latter experience.

Victims' responses and needs vary, especially if the crime was violent. Some victims may suffer a severe reaction immediately following the criminal offense; others may experience a delayed reaction, hours or even days after the offense. In either case, the severity of the individual victim's reaction will be proportional to his sense of violation or loss. Police officers should understand what triggers crisis reactions in victims in order to assist them. Officers should know that a burglary victim might have a very severe reaction, although he never saw the perpetrator, while an armed robbery victim who was actually confronted by the assailant might have a lesser reaction.

Police officers generally see victims and their families immediately after the crime, when they are most in need of help. The officers' response to these persons often has a major effect on how swiftly and how well the victim recovers. Police officers who respond quickly after the report is made, who listen attentively, and who show concern for the victim's plight will greatly reassure the victim and help him overcome his sense of fear and helplessness.

But good intentions on the part of police officers are not sufficient to assist every crime victim properly. Police officers need special training in "psychological first aid" [23] to help minimize victims' stress. Victims may experience depression, dependence, anger, a feeling of loss of control, guilt, or uncontrollable fear, either alone or in combination, and the response by the police must be both appropriate and sensitive.

Police officers also need special training to help them deal with crime victims. Victims become very frustrated when officers are not sensitive to their special circumstances. Police officers should not show skepticism because a rape victim is not badly bruised and bleeding or a child did not immediately report a molestation. Officers should be taught that elderly persons with sensory impairments are not necessarily senile and that blind persons can successfully assist the prosecution in criminal cases. They must be taught that family members of homicide victims need very much to be consulted and kept informed during the investigation, regardless of their ability to provide direct information.

Police officers must also learn to cope with their own job-related stress, so that they can effectively interact with victims.[24] Police officers are exposed to human misery daily, and may become very frustrated by their inability to resolve it fully. In order to compensate, some officers tend to minimize the problems of crime victims. This method of coping may help the officer in the short term, but it does a profound disservice to victims and will ultimately make the officer a less effective investigator.

The individual officer cannot be expected to meet each victim's needs personally and immediately, but he can serve as the essential link between the victim and the services that are available. This capacity is particularly important because officers see most victims, not just those whose cases result in arrest and prosecution. Some departments have cooperated with local churches or other volunteer groups who are available on call for counseling, death notification, and victim referral. In some departments, the police chaplain has been the motivating force behind this cooperation.[25]

Responsiveness to the needs of crime victims must be a departmental priority; as such, it should be an important part of every police officer's regular performance evaluation. A police department that rewards officers who assist crime victims either directly or through referral to a victim services program will greatly assist those who have been victimized. In addition, it can also help to reinforce the police officer's normal inclination to assist those victims who are in need of help.

For too long we have viewed the victim as evidentiary baggage to be carried to court along with blood samples and latent fingerprints. It is about time that we as police begin to view crime victims as our clients, as the aggrieved party in need of representation, reparation, and recognition.—Chief Robert P. Owens

This is one experience that one does not plan for, is not prepared for, has no knowledge of who or where to turn.—a victim

Police Recommendation 2:
Police departments should establish procedures for the prompt photographing and return of property to victims, with prosecutor approval.

60

My son's effects were never returned. My daughter wrote several letters, but to no avail. I presume they are lost to us forever. You can imagine how much the return of a gold chain my daughter had given him on his 17th birthday would have meant to her and how much the return of his wallet would have meant to me. The fact that no one was responsible for getting those items back to us hurt a great deal.—a victim's mother

The victim's property belongs to the victim, not the system. Victims repeatedly tell of property ranging from family heirlooms to an invalid's television set being held for months or years while the case moves slowly through the courts; in some cases, property has been mislaid or lost. Victims should have their property restored to them at the earliest date possible without compromising the prosecution of the case.

Police should cooperate with local prosecutors to develop procedures in which the prosecutor evaluates the evidentiary value of the property, notifies the defense, arranges inspection if necessary, then releases these items to their owners as expeditiously as possible (see Prosecutor Recommendation 6. Judicial responsibility is discussed in Judiciary Recommendation 9).

Departments must devise a system that will notify the victim or the victim's family when property has been recovered, where it is being held, when it can be reclaimed, and what documents must be presented when a claim is made. Before items are returned they should be photographed in a manner that clearly identifies the property and will allow substitution of the photograph for the item itself as an exhibit in court.

Police Recommendation 3:
Police departments should establish procedures to ensure that victims of violent crime are periodically informed of the status and closing of investigations.

Never once did local police direct me toward any means of assistance—no matter how loud I cried for help! I was even told it was none of my business when I asked the whereabouts of the defendants and the dates of the hearings. The defendants have "rights to privacy" according to my police department.—a victim

A major complaint voiced by victims is that they never hear anything about the case after the initial report. Further, when they attempt to acquire information by contacting the police, they are not able to give the names or numbers required for the police to locate the appropriate file. Even when an investigation is closed without an arrest, the victim should be so informed. Victims will appreciate police candor even when the case is unresolved.

Every victim of violent crime should be provided with certain basic information shortly after the crime is reported, either by mail or other satisfactory process. They should be told the name and badge number or department serial number of the investigator in charge of the case and how to reach him, the case number or other department data retrieval information, and when the case has been reassigned to a different investigator or branch within the department.

Many victims live in a state of fear, believing their assailant is still at large. When a suspect is apprehended, victims should be informed at the earliest possible time. This information can reduce their anxiety substantially. However, officers must take care not to compromise the reliability of a lineup or other investigatory phase by providing this information too soon; when in doubt, officers should consult with the prosecutor.

Police Recommendation 4:
Police officers should give a high priority to investigation of reports by witnesses of threats or intimidation and forward these reports to the prosecution.

Many victims and witnesses are threatened or intimidated by defendants and others. Fearing for themselves and their families, these citizens may move, begin to carry weapons, become prisoners in their homes, or decide not to follow through with the prosecution.

Although it may be difficult to ascertain who is responsible for these attempts at intimidation, officers must treat such threats and the citizens who are their targets with sensitivity and concern. It can be almost as frustrating for the officer as for the threatened person to realize the limitations inherent in this area. However, victims should not simply be told that nothing can be done; officers should respond to and investigate these reports.

In addition, some affirmative steps can be taken to protect those who are harassed and to give them the sense that the system is responsive to their problems (see also Prosecutors Recommendation 3). For example, traces or recordings can be arranged; the local precinct or beat supervisors can be alerted and the officers responsible for the victim's neighborhood can increase the frequency with which they patrol near the victim's home. Officers can inspect locks and instruct victims on how to improve their security measures. If victims decide to move, officers can ensure that they are not harassed or followed to their new

I was forced to take some drastic steps to protect myself. At first I blockaded myself in my apartment and began to carry a pistol. Later I moved to another city, got an unlisted phone number, used a post office box rather than my new address, and continued to carry a weapon. Even though I had done all of this, I still lived in fear.—a victim

residences. In jurisdictions in which investigating officers make recommendations as to bail, these attempts at intimidation should be brought to the attention of the court.

A formal report should be made every time a citizen complains of intimidation, and the victim should be referred to a victim/witness service provider. The filing of a formal report is important; it encourages the victim to remain in contact with law enforcement, and it documents a pattern of intimidation that can be proved at trial. If prosecutors are to succeed in opposing motions for release or reduction of bond, or if reports of harassment are to be relied on in sentencing, each threatening contact must be reported by the victim and documented in a formal report.

Recommendations for Prosecutors

The primary obligation of prosecutors is to see that truth and justice are served. The power of the prosecutor and the court system as a whole derives from the people's willingness to entrust to them the administration of justice. Prosecutors should keep their primary obligation in mind as they make decisions. In doing so they undertake the serious responsibility of serving the interests and concerns of citizens victimized by crime. These recommendations are meant to help prosecutors in this effort.

1. Prosecutors should assume ultimate responsibility for informing victims of the status of a case from the time of the initial charging decision to determinations of parole.
2. Prosecutors have an obligation to bring to the attention of the court the views of victims of violent crime on bail decisions, continuances, plea bargains, dismissals, sentencing, and restitution. They should establish procedures to ensure that such victims are given the opportunity to make their views on these matters known.
3. Prosecutors should charge and pursue to the fullest extent of the law defendants who harass, threaten, injure, or otherwise attempt to intimidate or retaliate against victims or witnesses.
4. Prosecutors should strongly discourage case continuances. When such delays are necessary, procedures should be established to ensure that cases are continued to dates agreeable to victims and witnesses, that those dates are secured in advance whenever possible, and that the reasons for the continuances are adequately explained.
5. Prosecutors' offices should use a victim and witness on-call system.
6. Prosecutors' offices should establish procedures to ensure the prompt return of victims' property, absent a need for the actual evidence in court.
7. Prosecutors' offices should establish and maintain direct liaison with victim/witness units and other victim service agencies.

8. Prosecutors must recognize the profound impact
that crimes of sexual violence have on both child
and adult victims and their families.

Commentary

Prosecutors Recommendation 1:
Prosecutors should assume ultimate responsibility for
informing victims of the status of a case from the time
of the initial charging decision to determinations of
parole.

I didn't hear anything about the case for almost a year. Then all of a sudden they called me up at work and said, "come down to court right away, the trial is going to take place."—a victim

The victim, not the state, is directly aggrieved by violent crime, and has an unquestionably valid interest in the prosecution his complaint initiates. Once a case is charged, the prosecutor is informed of all court dates, plea bargains, and rulings on pre-trial motions. The prosecutor is also in the best position to explain to victims the legal significance of various motions and proceedings.

Prosecutors should keep victims informed about the status of the case from the initial decision to charge or to decline prosecution. The only time a victim should not be informed of an aspect of a case is when the sharing of such information might improperly influence the victim's testimony or expose him to unnecessary attack on cross-examination.

Finally, my case was assigned to another district attorney who spent a great deal of time explaining to me what was happening in the case. Just being informed of all the facts reduced my anxiety greatly.—a victim

The prosecutor's duty to keep a victim of violent crime advised extends from the charging decision through sentencing and any subsequent parole hearings. The advisement of parole hearing dates is particularly important. Often victims do not realize that parole is even available to their assailant. When they are aware, they are often most interested in the outcome of parole hearings not only because of their desire for the service of a just sentence but also because of their legitimate fear of revictimization once the defendant is released.

Better treatment of victims should be a high priority for prosecutors. Ensuring that victims of violent crimes are advised of the progress of their case is only a beginning in the recognition of this responsibility.

Prosecutors Recommendation 2:

Prosecutors have an obligation to bring to the attention of the court the views of victims of violent crimes on bail decisions, continuances, plea bargains, dismissals, sentencing, and restitution. They should establish procedures to ensure that such victims are given the opportunity to make their views on these matters known.

Prosecutors must champion the public interest while respecting the rights of the accused. They must also serve victims by ensuring that they will not be victimized again, either by the criminal or the system that was designed to protect the innocent. Ordinarily, victims are unaware of how the system operates; they do not understand its complex processes and are troubled by their apparent exclusion from participation in the adjudication of a case that so directly affects them. Not only must the system be explained to them, but they must also be allowed to convey the information that they possess to those making the decisions that will determine the outcome of the case. The prosecutor not only has direct victim contact, but he is also in the best position to see that the victim is accorded a proper role in the criminal justice system.

Prosecutors are often unaware, at the time of the bail hearing, that threats of reprisal have been made to victims, either because the police did not obtain this information or because the threats were made after the investigation was completed. It is difficult for a judge to evaluate the danger that a defendant presents to the community if the judge hears only from the defendant's counsel, who will present him in the best possible light, and from a prosecutor who does not know of the basis for the victim's fear. Also, it is not uncommon for a suspect to tell the victim of his intention to flee should he be released. The person best able to inform the court of statements that may have been made by the defendant and the threat he poses is often the person he victimized.

As is discussed elsewhere (see Prosecutors Recommendation 4 and Judiciary Recommendation 4), continuances impose a substantial hardship on victims and often undermine the prosecution's case. Postponements should be opposed whenever possible. If a continuance is granted, the prosecutor should inform the court of any conflicts with the victim's schedule.

Victims responded that they wanted to be included, consulted, and informed, regardless of their usefulness to the prosecution, regardless of whether their case was plea bargained, dismissed, or brought to trial.—Deborah Kelly

With the court process there is no guarantee of a light at the end of a tunnel. Life plans are put on hold indefinitely and the victim merely treads water.—Gail Pisarcik

What others see as an inconvenience is for the victim an endless nightmare.—a victim

Prosecutors should consult with every victim of violent crime, explaining how the plea bargaining system operates, what negotiating posture the prosecution has adopted, and why that posture was chosen. Prosecutors should always take into account the victim's views before reaching a final decision. Although lawyers and judges rely on plea bargaining as a tool of calendar management, victims legitimately view the resolution of and sentencing in a case as an evaluation of the harm done to them.

Whenever the prosecutor considers the dismissal of a case involving violent crime, the victim should be consulted in advance and told the reasons for the prosecutor's decision.

Two lives—the defendant's and the victim's—are profoundly affected by a criminal sentence. The court cannot make an informed decision on a just punishment if it hears from only one side. Justice demands that victims be allowed to inform the court in writing and in person of the nature of the crime and the full effect that it has had on them and their families. Prosecutors have a responsibility to ensure that victims of violent crime are informed of the pre-sentencing report process, that victims have the opportunity to have their views reflected in those reports, and that victims have the opportunity to appear and be heard at the time of sentencing.

Restitution should be ordered in every case in which the victim has suffered monetary loss (see Judiciary Recommendation 7). Prosecutors should inform victims of the availability of restitution as a sentencing option for the court, assist victims in outlining their financial losses to the compilers of the pre-sentence report, and ensure that the court is made aware of the victim's losses so that a restitution order is accurate and inclusive. Prosecutors should consider the issue of restitution for the victim in charging and plea bargaining decisions, which may affect the amount of restitution the court can order.

Prosecutors Recommendation 3:
Prosecutors should charge and pursue to the fullest extent of the law defendants who harass, threaten, injure, or otherwise attempt to intimidate or retaliate against victims or witnesses.

Victims and witnesses are threatened or harassed far more frequently than prosecutors are aware (see also Police Recommendation 4). [26] This activity continues the process of victimization and confirms one of the victim's worst fears, that the system cannot protect him; he may feel that the only way to escape reprisal is to refuse to testify. The Task Force recognizes that it may often be difficult to file charges of witness intimidation. There may be no identifiable perpetrator for the anonymous call in the night or for seemingly random violence and vandalism directed at a victim or witness. But when a suspect is identified, prosecutors must charge and prosecute vigorously. Harassment and intimidation strike at the very heart of the truth-finding process. By failing to prosecute, dismissing cases or not requesting that terms for intimidation be served consecutively, prosecutors, perhaps inadvertently, convey many messages. Criminals may perceive that intimidation is worth a try—it may succeed, and there is no risk of further punishment. In addition, victims and witnesses may perceive that they are on their own, that they will not be protected by the system that already asks so much of them.

After the assault, I spent only one night in the residence we had shared for most of our 48 years of married life. I was persuaded to move when my youngest daughter answered the phone and was advised by the caller to withdraw the charges.—a victim

Prosecutors Recommendation 4:
Prosecutors should strongly discourage case continuances. When such delays are necessary, procedures should be established to ensure that cases are continued to dates agreeable to victims and witnesses, that those dates are secured in advance whenever possible, and that the reasons for the continuances are adequately explained.

Continuances in criminal proceedings can by their very nature prolong and intensify the initial victimization. The effect on victims' schedules, obligations, and lives can be both bewildering and profound. Continuances are used to good advantage by the defense; they can result in the ultimate unavailability of some witnesses and the fading memory of others.

Prosecutors can be as irresponsible as any other participant in the system in seeking continuances for their own convenience without considering the effect these delays have on the victimized. Victims must be allowed to put their experience behind them as soon as possible. They also should not be required to incur

Each time after a continuance, I would sink back down in the hole. I spent two years not knowing what was going to happen to me.—a victim

the cost and inconvenience of arranging for child care, taking time off from work, and missing vacations and breaking appointments only to discover that the case will not be heard.

Prosecutors should vigorously oppose continuances except when they are necessary for the accomplishment of legitimate investigatory procedures or to accommodate the scheduling needs of victims. (See also Judiciary Recommendation 4 and The Bar Recommendation 1). Whenever possible it should be determined in advance if a continuance is to be granted and the victim should be informed.

Prosecutors Recommendation 5:
Prosecutors' offices should use an on-call system for victims and witnesses.

I worked second shift and this meant I had to go to court all day from morning to afternoon, then go from court to work all evening. I could not afford to lose the time from work. It was like working two jobs, and was very difficult for me and my family.—a victim

Prosecutors and courts should cooperate in implementing an effective on-call and notification system (see also Judiciary Recommendation 2). It is seldom excusable or necessary for witnesses to appear, ready to cooperate, only to be told to leave and return another day. By allowing victims and witnesses to fulfill their regular obligations while on call, the system can minimize inconvenience, wage loss, and other hardships. In addition, such a system can save revenues and increase the efficiency of government services by reducing witness fees and police officer overtime pay, while increasing the time officers spend at other duties.

Prosecutors Recommendation 6:
Prosecutors' offices should establish procedures to ensure the prompt return of victims' property, absent a need for the actual evidence in court.

When a criminal takes their property, victims should not have to battle the justice system to get it back or wait for months or years for its return (see also Police Recommendation 2 and Judiciary Recommendation 9). Naturally there will be some items that will have particular evidentiary significance, whether seized from the defendant or taken from the victim or crime scene, because of their character or condition. These must be retained for admission at trial. Other items, however, can be presented to the jury just as effectively by photograph. If the chain of custody is not an issue, such items can be kept and used by victims while the case proceeds, rather than being kept in a police or court clerk's property room. Early return is also cost effective, relieving government of the expense of storage.

Prosecutors must of course weigh evidentiary considerations and allow the defense an opportunity to view and examine victims' property. In taking these steps, the prosecutor should recognize his responsibility to release property as expeditiously as possible, to take the initiative in doing so, and to establish the procedures necessary to bring about the expeditious restoration of property to its lawful owner.

I kept trying to get my property back, the property that they had for court evidence. But no one could tell me where it was. I was sent to warehouses, government offices, and made phone call after phone call before I finally got back some of the things the authorities had all along.—a victim

Prosecutors Recommendation 7:
Prosecutors' offices should establish and maintain direct liaison with victim/witness units and other victim service agencies.

Victims cannot rely on services they know nothing about. Prosecutors must make themselves aware of the victim/witness services that are available and ensure that victims are informed of them. The prosecutor should extend this information because he is a public servant; in addition, the prosecution will profit from the better cooperation of a victim who feels he has been protected and assisted. The prosecutor should consider offering training to area victim service providers on the workings of the criminal justice system. He should also consider inviting people outside the criminal justice system who work directly with crime victims to discuss victims' needs and their perceptions of how the prosecutor is or is not meeting these needs with his staff.

Prosecutors Recommendation 8:
Prosecutors must recognize the profound impact that crimes of sexual violence have on both child and adult victims and their families.

In recent years some prosecutors have improved greatly in the manner in which they treat sexual assault victims (see also Judiciary Recommendation 10). Unfortunately, however, substantial progress remains to be made. Myths, superstitions, and prejudices are

I feel that we all tolerate sexual abuse of children as long as we accept a criminal justice system that victimizes children instead of making changes to help the child who must endure this ordeal.—Lorna Bernhard

The problems began when the prosecutors said that any child under the age of seven could not qualify as a witness. They refused to sit down and speak to my daugher about the facts of the case. The detectives who interviewed her thought that she could qualify as a witness at trial and do an excellent job.—a victim

being eradicated much too slowly. Sexual assault victims must be treated with the same respect and compassion due anyone victimized by crime. Further, the emotional dimension of their victimization requires that they be treated with particular care. Practices that reflect distrust of these victims, such as polygraph testing of rape victims or the implementation of separate charging procedures in the evaluation of their cases, must stop. In terms of case disposition, plea bargaining, and sentence recommendations, the prosecutor's attitude must reflect a concern for the violent nature of any sexual assault and the danger posed by anyone who would engage in such conduct.

Many prosecutors fail to treat child molestation cases with the seriousness they deserve. The profound trauma inflicted on young victims and the after effects that may mar them for life are simply immeasurable. Those who impose this activity on children are dangerous and will continue to be so. Witnesses who are experienced in this field have informed the Task Force that those who engage in sex with children do so by choice, not as the uncontrollable by-product of some disease. Because their conduct is purposeful and there is little motivation for change, treatment is usually unsuccessful. The most recent data suggest that this conduct will continue throughout the molester's life and will escalate as he ages.[27]

These individuals represent a continuing threat to children. Prosecutors should be taking the lead in making them accountable for their conduct. Yet molesters have a better chance than most criminals of escaping detection and successful prosecution. Children often fail to report these occurrences to their parents because of the attacker's threats, because they are embarrassed, or because they fear their parents will be angry. If their parents are told, they may elect not to inform authorities because they are embarrassed, confused, wish to deny the problem, or think they should protect their children from the effects of involvement in the criminal justice system.

When prosecutors do get such cases, they may be hesitant to charge or anxious to plea bargain because these cases are often difficult to try. The prosecutor will often seize on parental reticence as an excuse not to proceed with the case instead of working with the parents to determine what course is best for the child and for the protection of future victims.

Prosecutors must take the time to explain the court process to children and to prepare them for it. In these cases, continuances should be kept to the absolute minimum because the delay is particularly difficult for children and because delay weakens the prosecution's case as young memories fade.

It is essential that prosecutors urge in plea bargaining or in post-conviction sentence hearings that these offenders be sequestered from the public. Treatment can always be tried, but it should, rarely if ever, be the sole remedy.

A 19-year-old molested my daughter in a day-care center. He had a prior conviction for similar behavior. The prosecutor asked for 8 years in prison. The judge gave him 90 days, saying he might be harassed in custody.—a victim

Recommendations for the Judiciary

The ultimate responsibility for how the system operates rests with judges, who must reconfirm their dedication to be fair to both sides of a criminal prosecution. If they fail to do this, they do not serve the public from whom their authority is derived. In passing judgment, from initial bail hearing to the imposition of a sentence that properly reflects the seriousness of the offense, to appellate review of convictions and sentences, each jurist must act with the goal of equal justice clearly in mind. These recommendations are meant to help keep that goal clear.

1. It should be mandatory that judges at both the trial and appellate level participate in a training program addressing the needs and legal interests of crime victims.

2. Judges should allow victims and witnesses to be on call for court proceedings.

3. Judges or their court administrators should establish separate waiting rooms for prosecution and defense witnesses.

4. When ruling on requests for continuances, judges should give the same weight to the interests of victims and witnesses as that given to the interests of defendants. Further, judges should explain the basis for such rulings on the record.

5. Judges should bear their share of responsibility for reducing court congestion by ensuring that all participants fully and responsibly utilize court time.

6. Judges should allow for, and give appropriate weight to, input at sentencing from victims of violent crime.

7. Judges should order restitution to the victim in all cases in which the victim has suffered financial loss, unless they state compelling reasons for a contrary ruling on the record.

8. Judges should allow the victim and a member of the victim's family to attend the trial, even if identified as witnesses, absent a compelling need to the contrary.

9. Judges should give substantial weight to the victim's interest in speedy return of property before trial in ruling on the admissibility of photographs of that property.

10. Judges should recognize the profound impact that sexual molestation of children has on victims and their families and treat it as a crime that should result in punishment, with treatment available when appropriate.

Commentary

Judiciary Recommendation 1:
It should be mandatory that judges at both the trial and appellate level participate in a training program addressing the needs and legal interests of crime victims.

The courtroom is the focal point of the entire criminal justice system. The work of police, prosecutors, and defense attorneys is all in preparation for the presentation of the case in court. Most trials are conducted with consideration given to any appeal that may ensue. The judge who presides over a court becomes not only the final arbiter of each evidentiary and procedural issue, but he also establishes the tone, the pace, and the very nature of the proceedings. Particularly for the victim, the judge is the personification of justice. The victim may have been badly treated by police, doctors, lawyers, even neighbors and co-workers, but he expects that finally the judge will accord him just treatment.

Often judges are not prepared to meet this expectation. Those who come to the bench from a civil practice, or even those who have been advocates for one side or the other in the criminal justice system, may lack the experience and insight required to understand the victim's view. On a broader level, a judge is no longer an advocate, yet his previous experience may result in a natural inclination to approach the issues from a particular perspective. Justice requires an informed impartiality. Fair evaluation of courtroom arguments requires that the judge have some insight into the human experience those arguments address.

Judges must *take a stronger hand in controlling their calendars. They must be as concerned with inconveniences to victims and witnesses as they are with inconveniences to attorneys. Too often the system appears to operate for the benefit of the court and attorneys.—Judge Marilyn Hall Patel*

74

To this end, judges from the magistrate to appellate and Supreme Court levels should be required to undergo a program of training before they assume the bench. To avoid a tendency to become insular in their thinking, judges should receive periodic training during their tenure.

Justice requires extraordinary vigilance lest it become too removed from those who depend on the equity of its processes. A practical course of instruction during which judges ride along with police, see victims at the scene, view local line-up procedures, inspect interview facilities and jail and prison conditions, and take courses that address the particular needs and legal interests of victims will enable judges to attain more closely the level of justice to which they aspire.

Judiciary Recommendation 2:
Judges should allow victims and witnesses to be on call for court proceedings.

To avoid an occasional brief delay in court proceedings, many judges require all victims and witnesses to be present before they will begin litigation. This requirement is both unnecessary and burdensome. All witnesses need not attend the entire proceeding; they need appear only when their testimony is called for. It is certainly unfair and inefficient to have them all assemble, only to be told that the case will be continued, or to sit and wait for hours or days while a jury is selected and pre-trial legal issues are resolved. In this era of instant communication and rapid transit, it is more equitable, more efficient, and less burdensome to allow victims and witnesses to remain at their jobs or in their homes until the actual need for their participation is reasonably imminent. Judges and prosecutors should cooperate in determining the need for victims' and witnesses' presence in court (see Prosecutors Recommendation 5). An additional benefit derived is the savings in payment of witness fees and the cost of police overtime.

Judiciary Recommendation 3:
Judges or their court administrators should establish separate waiting rooms for prosecution and defense witnesses.

There is a natural antipathy between the victim and the defendant, his family, and friends. The victim may be fearful; he was brutalized during the crime, often was threatened afterward, and now must stand alone and identify the person who committed the offense. This requirement is difficult enough in the relative protection of the courtroom. Victims and witnesses should not be required to sit and wait with the defendant and his supporters. At the very least, this is an awkward and disturbing human encounter; at the worst, it becomes the breeding ground for threats, intimidation and violence.

We had to sit outside the courtroom, where there was only one chair, sometimes in the presence of the man who was charged with doing this and his family. There was no separate place for victims and witnesses.—a victim

Judiciary Recommendation 4:
When ruling on requests for continuances, judges should give the same weight to the interests of victims and witnesses as that given to the interests of defendants. Further, judges should explain the basis for such rulings on the record.

Parties seek continuances for a variety of reasons. Some are justified, many are not. It is the responsibility of the judge to ensure that criminal cases are resolved as expeditiously as possible because victims are profoundly affected by case delays. The defendant has a right to a speedy trial, not only because he may be incarcerated while it is pending, but also because of the hardship inherent in having criminal charges unresolved. Victims likewise are burdened by irresolution and the realization that they will be called upon to relieve their victimization when the case is finally tried. The healing process cannot truly begin until the case can be put behind them. This is especially so for children and victims of sexual assault or any other case involving violence.

People have to realize that emotional scabs are constantly being scraped off as you appear time after time in court.—a victim

In recognition of these factors, continuances should be granted sparingly and only for good cause. Lawyers must be required to conduct their practices efficiently, and courts must employ sound calendar management procedures. Judges must be aware that lawyers on both sides try to manipulate the continuance system for their own ends, ends that serve neither the victim nor the interests of justice (see also Prosecutors Recommendation 4 and the Bar Recommendation 1). Only the court can ensure that such improper manipulation is avoided. Because this Task Force recognizes

Judges should take responsibility for explaining to the victims the reasons for the continuance. I suggest that where a judge is required to explain those reasons to a waiting victim the reasons will often appear less persuasive.—Judge Marilyn Hall Patel

the importance of this issue and the manner in which it so severely affects victims, and because we recognize the inherent human tendency to postpone matters, often for insufficient reason, we urge that the reasons for any granted continuance and the identification of the party requesting it be clearly stated on the record.

Judiciary Recommendation 5:
Judges should bear their share of responsibility for reducing court congestion by ensuring that all participants fully and responsibly utilize court time.

Then we were told that the trial must be rescheduled for August because the judge could not hear a 5-day trial and still keep an important speaking engagement.—a victim

Criminal cases may take a long time to try. Some of this delay cannot be avoided; the fair determination of truth cannot be rushed. However, judges must set an appropriate pace and require that participants keep to it. Proceedings must start on time, and court hours must be effectively used. Both witnesses and advocates have had experience with courts that do not convene until midmorning or that recess in midafternoon. Occasionally such measures are necessary to coordinate schedules or to allow the informed argument of legal issues. But such practices cannot be allowed to become the norm to accommodate judges' personal schedules. Judges must begin their days on time and expect those who appear before them to arrive promptly and to be prepared.

Judiciary Recommendation 6:
Judges should allow for, and give appropriate weight to, input at sentencing from victims of violent crime.

Balancing competing interests and equities in deciding a sentence can require a Solomon-like wisdom—and even Solomon heard from both sides.—a victim

The imposition of a criminal penalty may be the most difficult kind of decision a judge is called on to make. In addition to affecting the defendant, the sentence is a barometer of the seriousness with which the criminal conduct is viewed. It is also a statement of social disapprobation, a warning to those tempted to emulate the offender's actions, and a step that must be taken for the protection of society. Finally, it is a statement of societal concern to the victim for what he has endured.

Victims, no less than defendants, are entitled to their day in court. Victims, no less than defendants, are entitled to have their views considered. A judge cannot evaluate the seriousness of a defendant's conduct without knowing how the crime has burdened the victim. A judge cannot reach an informed determination of the danger posed by a defendant without hearing from the person he has victimized (see Executive and Legislative Recommendation 10, which would require the filing of victim impact statements).

Victims of violent crime should be allowed to provide information at two levels. One, the victim should be permitted to inform the person preparing the presentence report of the circumstances and consequences of the crime. Any recommendation on sentencing that does not consider such information is simply one-sided and inadequate. Two, every victim must be allowed to speak at the time of sentencing. The victim, no less than the defendant, comes to court seeking justice. When the court hears, as it may, from the defendant, his lawyer, his family and friends, his minister, and others, simple fairness dictates that the person who has borne the brunt of the defendant's crime be allowed to speak.

I personally feel that it is a miscarriage of justice to sentence a defendant who has been convicted of committing a crime against another person without first hearing from the victim and taking into account the effects the crime has had on the victim's life.—Judge Reggie Walton

The idea that the victim should speak at sentencing has been met with resistance. That opposition and the force with which it has been projected by judges and lawyers is one measure of their lack of concern for victims. It is also an indication of how much is wrong with the sentencing system.

The Task Force has found that in seeking to defend what is, in the final analysis, the indefensible view that victims have no right to participate in the sentencing of their victimizers, lawyers and judges often rely on two primary arguments. First, they assert that victim participation will take too much time—but from the charging process through the trial and the entire post-sentence process, tremendous amounts of time and effort are expended to safeguard the rights of the defendant. The pre-sentence report process is almost exclusively aimed at evaluating each nuance of the defendant's background and current position. Defendants speak and are spoken for often at great length, before sentence is imposed. It is outrageous that the system should contend it is too busy to hear from the victim.

Others may speculate about the defendant's potential for violence; it is the victim who looked down the barrel of the gun, or felt his blows, or knew how serious were the threats of death that the defendant conveyed. Friends or relatives may speak of the defendant's newfound remorse; it is the victim who can tell of the defendant's response to his pleas to be spared, to be hurt no further. It is the victim who knows how the defendant said he would avoid capture or dupe the judge if he were caught. The defendant comes to court to convince the judge he is loved and supported by family and friends. What of the family and friends of the murder victim, who was no less loved and supported, no less needed, and who is no less dead at the defendant's hand?

The victim was there when the crime was committed; at the very least, he and his family have had to rebuild their lives in its aftermath. A few minutes to help the court understand the personal effect of the defendant's lawlessness seems little to ask. The impact of the crime on the victim's physical, financial, and psychological well-being must be explained.

The second argument is that participation by victims at sentencing will place improper pressure on judges. The duty of a judge is to dispense justice, and the passing of judgment is a difficult task. The difficulty of the task should not be relieved, however, by discharging it unfairly. Hearing from the defendant and his family and looking into the faces of his children while passing sentence is not easy, but no one could responsibly suggest that the defendant be denied his right to be heard or suffer a sentence imposed in secret in order to spare the judge. The victim, no less than the defendant, has a real and personal interest in seeing the imposition of a just penalty. The goal of victim participation is not to pressure justice, but to aid in its attainment. The judge cannot take a balanced view if his information is acquired from only one side. The prosecutor can begin to present the other side, but he was not personally affected by the crime or its aftermath, and may not be fully aware of the price the victim has paid. It is as unfair to require that the victim depend solely on the intercession of the prosecutor as it would be to require that the defendant rely solely on his counsel.

In putting the man who robbed me on probation, the judge said he had suffered enough by being tried and losing his job. I was put through the system, too. I lost my job. The big difference between us is he chose to rob me; I didn't choose to be a victim.—a victim

Judiciary Recommendation 7:
Judges should order restitution to the victim in all cases in which the victim has suffered financial loss,

unless they state compelling reasons for a contrary ruling on the record.

Crime exacts a tremendous economic cost. In the vast majority of cases it is the victim, not the offender, who eventually shoulders this burden. This is unjust. The concept of personal accountability for the consequences of one's conduct, and the allied notion that the person who causes the damage should bear the cost, are at the heart of civil law. It should be no less true in criminal law.

It is simply unfair that victims should have to liquidate their assets, mortgage their homes, or sacrifice their health or education or that of their children while the offender escapes responsibility for the financial hardship he has imposed. It is unjust that a victim should have to sell his car to pay bills while the offender drives to his probation appointments. The victim may be placed in a financial crisis that will last a lifetime. If one of the two must go into debt, the offender should do so.

In addition, the court should accept responsibility for enforcing its restitution orders. Courts should require meaningful progress reports on whether the defendant is meeting his obligations. If the offender misses payments, this fact should be brought to the attention of the court in a timely fashion. A court should rarely find itself confronting a situation in which the probation of an offender who is delinquent in his restitution payments is about to expire. Probation or parole should seldom be terminated until the restitution obligation has been met.

A restitution order should be imposed in every case in which a financial loss is suffered, whether or not the defendant is incarcerated. Neither victims nor courts should be forced to choose between restraining a violent and dangerous offender or making the victim economically whole. If payment cannot begin before the offender's release, such delay is still preferable to no payment at all. Many offenders receive financial benefits while in custody; some states allow prisoners to be paid wages for work while serving a sentence, and others are considering adopting such a policy.[28] In the rare instances in which restitution is

I think if the criminals who do these things are caught they should have to pay for the damage they do, even if it takes them years. My family and I will be trying to recover from this for the rest of our lives.—a victim

The man who murdered my husband is in prison, thankfully. We as taxpayers are paying for his room, board, and medical and psychiatric help. My husband was my only means of support. I'm now destitute, very ill, and have no financial means. Meanwhile, the murderer has 600 acres of valuable property. Why should the man who ruined my life be able to keep and return in a few years to that, while I have nothing?—a victim

not ordered, judges should state clearly and specifically, on the record, the reasons why they did not so order.

Judiciary Recommendation 8:
Judges should allow the victim and a member of the victim's family to attend the trial, even if identified as witnesses, absent a compelling need to the contrary.

Judges are responsible for maintaining the integrity of the truth-finding process. One way this has been done is by excluding witnesses from the courtroom so that their testimony could not be influenced by their observations. However, this procedure can be abused by advocates and can impose an improper hardship on victims and their relatives. Time and again, we heard from victims or their families that they were unreasonably excluded from the trial at which responsibility for their victimization was assigned. This is especially difficult for the families of murder victims and for witnesses who are denied the supportive presence of parents or spouses during their testimony.

The crime is often one of the most significant events in the lives of victims and their families. They, no less than the defendant, have a legitimate interest in the fair adjudication of the case, and should therefore, as an exception to the general rule providing for the exclusion of witnesses, be permitted to be present for the entire trial.

Testifying can be a harrowing experience, especially for children, those subjected to violent or terrifying ordeals, or those whose loved ones have been murdered. These witnesses often need the support provided by the presence of a family member or loved one, but these persons are often excluded if the defense has designated them as witnesses. Sometimes those designations are legitimate; on other occasions they are only made to confuse or disturb the opposition. We suggest that the fairest balance between the need to support both witnesses and defendants and the need to prevent the undue influence of testimony lies in allowing a designated individual to be present regardless of his status as a witness. If this individual does finally testify, his presence throughout the trial is a valid subject for comment by the opposition and may be a subject that the court addresses during jury instructions.

I was not allowed to watch the trial because the defense attorney subpoenaed me as a witness. There was no real reason for me to be subpoenaed other than to keep me out of the trial. His intentions were also made apparent by the fact that he gave me the subpoena even though he had never interviewed me and would not have known what I might have said if he called me to testify. As was expected, I never was called to testify by the defense at the trial.— a victim

Judiciary Recommendation 9:
Judges should give substantial weight to the victim's interest in speedy return of property before trial in ruling on the admissibility of photographs of that property.

We have recommended elsewhere (see Police Recommendation 2 and Prosecutors Recommendation 6) that, whenever possible, property should be photographed and returned to victims expeditiously. This can happen only if courts will allow the substitution of photographs, properly identified through testimony, for the television sets, silver services, and other items that would otherwise be witheld from victims until the case is tried and the appellate process completed. There will be instances in which the property itself must be admitted because of its character, condition, or questions about the chain of custody; however, in many cases the admission of a photograph is just as satisfactory as the admission of the actual object. In fact, not only is the victim well served by return of his property, but the system is also spared the cost of its storage.

Judiciary Recommendation 10:
Judges should recognize the profound impact that sexual molestation of children has on victims and their families and treat it as a crime that should result in punishment, with treatment available when appropriate.

Perhaps no crime is more misunderstood and less adequately treated by the criminal justice system than the sexual molestation of children (see also Prosecutor Recommendation 8). Everyone who confronts these cases finds them difficult. There is almost a need to find that the conduct is the result of mistake, misinterpretation, or psychological aberration. Yet denial only exacerbates a problem that has reached almost epidemic proportions in this country.[29] Thousands of innocent children every year pay the price for this denial.

Children who are victimized in this way, even if they are not physically injured, may be harmed severely, perhaps more severely than any other victim. The effects on them and on their families are profound. Yet the sentences imposed for this conduct are

You can't say pedophilia is an illness any more than you can say bank robbery is an illness. Treatment has been used as an escape from responsibility.— Roland Summit, Ph. D.

generally inappropriate and are significantly lower than terms imposed for adult rape.[30] It is appalling to read of a judge who says a 5-year old was sexually promiscuous.[31] It is unconscionable that someone who molested a child in a day-care center was sentenced to a month or two in the county jail.

The best psychiatric findings indicate that these defendants are responsible for their conduct, and that treatment in this area is rarely successful.[32] Those who engage in sex with children do so because they choose to, and they will continue to make that choice as long as they are free to do so with impunity. Those who prey on children must be sequestered from them. They may be incarcerated in hospitals, treatment centers, or prisons; but wherever they are held, they must not be released until they have served a sentence that is commensurate with the harm they have inflicted.

Recommendations for Parole Boards

Parole boards should be abolished. They operate in secret and without accountability; they release the dangerous, who prey upon the innocent. (See also Executive and Legislative recommendations 6 and 7.) Post-release supervision is both inadequate and tremendously costly. Until such time as this system is replaced, the recommendations below may help correct the more dangerous abuses.

1. **Parole boards should notify victims of crime and their families in advance of parole hearings, if names and addresses have been previously provided by these individuals.**
2. **Parole boards should allow victims of crime, their families, or their representatives to attend parole hearings and make known the effect of the offender's crime on them.**
3. **Parole boards should take whatever steps are necessary to ensure that parolees charged with a crime while on parole are immediately returned to custody and kept there until the case is adjudicated.**
4. **Parole boards should not apply the exclusionary rule to parole revocation hearings.**

Commentary

Parole Board Recomendations 1 and 2:
(1) Parole boards should notify victims of crime and their families in advance of parole hearings, if names and addresses have been previously provided by these individuals; (2) Parole boards should allow victims of crime, their families, or their representatives to attend parole hearings and make known the effect of the offender's crime on them.

The essence of responsibility is accountability. Many parole board abuses stem from the fact that their decisions are arrived at behind closed doors. Parole decisions in recent years seem to be based on the supposition that only the prisoner is affected. Nothing could be more erroneous. Although a prisoner's behavior while incarcerated should be considered in parole decisions, the nature of his conduct while at large is vital. No one knows better than the victim how dangerous and ruthless the candidate was before he was subjected to the scrutiny of the parole board.

Society has taken on itself the responsibility for protecting the innocent and punishing the guilty. This responsibility must be fairly discharged. Victims have a legitimate interest in seeing not only that their attackers are appropriately punished but also that they are not released prematurely to harm others.

If a prisoner is to be released, victims should be notified in advance. The victim may have been threatened during or after the crime, or may be seen by the prisoner as the one responsible for the prisoner's incarceration. Victims' fear of retaliation is deep and real. They should be allowed to take precautions or at the very least prepare themselves mentally for the release of their victimizers.

I also feel that I should be allowed at the parole hearings or be allowed to send a representative. I think it would be very difficult for me to attend them; but I feel that it should be my right to have the option.—a victim

Parole Board Recommendation 3:

Parole boards should take whatever steps are necessary to ensure that parolees charged with a crime while on parole are immediately returned to custody and kept there until the case is adjudicated.

The local parole board has resisted our legitimate attempts to voice our position at initial parole hearings involving dangerous and repeat offenders. Undoubtedly, if the parole board were more concerned with the plight of crime victims, the streets would be safer and the need for witness protection would be reduced.—Stanley S. Harris, United States Attorney

The release of a prisoner on parole involves a judgment by the releasing authority that the convict does not pose a criminal threat and that he has knowingly agreed to abide by the law. The parolee's commission of a new crime requires that responsible action be taken by the parole board to restore the safety of the community. Although the legal presumption of innocence still applies, the rearrest of the prisoner, followed by a judicial finding of probable cause, should raise grave doubts about the wisdom of allowing the parolee to remain in the community. It should always be borne in mind that a new victim has paid the price for the parolee's release. Paroled prisoners who are rearrested should be held in custody until culpability for the new crime is resolved at either a trial or parole revocation hearing.

Parole Board Recommendation 4:
Parole boards should not apply the exclusionary rule to parole revocation hearings.

We have already discussed elsewhere in this report our complete dissatisfaction with the exclusionary rule and have recommended that it be abolished (see Executive and Legislative Recommendation 7). Until that is accomplished, however, the exclusionary rule should not be used by any parole boards in parole revocation hearings.

Parole boards that have adopted the exclusionary rule refuse to consider clear violations of parole simply because of a police officer's mistake. These parole boards have taken this position in spite of numerous court decisions that have made it clear that the exclusionary rule is not legally required in parole hearings.[33] Their use of the exclusionary rule is therefore a matter of choice and not a legal requirement.

Our recommendation was reached by balancing competing interests: the innocent victim's need for protection and the interests of a person who has been convicted of an offense, imprisoned, and granted the privilege of early conditional release, which he has clearly violated. The strength of our conclusion is apparent. Parole boards have an obligation to protect the community. They can no longer in good conscience grant early release to a parolee and then close their eyes to obvious violations of the parole privilege. To do otherwise shows flagrant disregard of the needs of victims and the community.

Accordingly, parole boards must consider revocation of parole when the facts show clearly that parole has been violated.

Recommendations for Other Organizations

Recommendations for Other Organizations

It is obvious that the criminal justice system and the actions of its agents directly affect victims. Less evident, perhaps, are the effects of agencies outside that system with which victims must also deal, particularly hospitals, the ministry, the bar, and the school system. These recommendations are meant to help those agencies assist victims of crime more effectively.

Recommendations for Hospitals

Finding oneself in need of medical treatment is always unsettling. When crime victims need medical treatment, they bring with them problems that may exceed their injuries. In addition to their physical condition, they are often fearful and insecure. Hospital staff members who are indifferent and treat the patient with insensitivity increase rather than diminish the patient's trauma, and may ultimately impede the overall healing process. The following recommendations are meant to ensure that hospitals are as helpful as possible to victims of crime.

1. Hospitals should establish and implement training programs for hospital personnel to sensitize them to the needs of victims of violent crimes, especially the elderly and those who have been sexually assaulted.
2. Hospitals should provide emergency medical assistance to victims of violent crime without regard to their ability to pay, and collect payments from state victim compensation programs.
3. Hospitals should provide emergency room crisis counseling to victims of crime and their families.
4. Hospitals should encourage and develop direct liaison with all victim assistance and social service agencies.
5. Hospitals should develop, in consultation with prosecuting agencies, a standardized rape kit for proper collection of physical evidence, and develop a procedure to ensure proper storage and maintenance of such evidence until it is released to the appropriate agency.

Commentary

Hospitals Recommendation 1:
Hospitals should establish and implement training programs for hospital personnel to sensitize them to the needs of victims of violent crime, especially the elderly and those who have been sexually assaulted.

Emergency rooms, especially in urban areas, are often overcrowded, understaffed, and hectic. For the victim of violence, sitting for hours in a hospital waiting room can magnify the already substantial trauma of the crime. It is understandable and necessary that hospitals give priority to treatment of life-threatening injury. However, violent crime often imposes serious psychological trauma even when the attendant physical injuries are superficial. Testimony before this Task Force demonstrated convincingly that ignoring those emotional wounds can render almost meaningfuless any restoration of physical health and may even inhibit the healing process.

Hospitals must train and require their staffs to respond sensitively to the needs of crime victims. Those responsible for notifying a victim's family of death or injury must be made aware of the delicacy of this task. Unfortunately, the two victim experiences described below were disturbingly representative.

> My mother . . . was notified by the hospital that my 66-year-old father was there, having met with an unfortunate accident, and was in critical condition. The hospital refused to tell her any details of how seriously injured he was . . . . What they did question her at length about was their financial status, hospitalization, the amount of his pension, and how much social security he received. What I want to know is did they know that he was going to die [from his gunshot wounds] when they were saying all this to her?

> . . . Late that night we were called by [the police] and told our daughter had been shot in the head, but that any other details would have to come from the hospital. After many calls to the hospital and the police, a doctor came on the line and announced, "She's dead." That's how we learned of our daughter's murder.

Training should be largely directed at emergency room doctors, nurses, and other personnel because they frequently see victims and their families during periods of acute emotional stress. Because turnover in

If blood is freeflowing you get attention quickly and it is seen as a serious problem. Attending to emotional wounds is a much more difficult process.—Emily Chandler

I was taken to city hospital where I waited approximately three hours before I was treated. I was angry and it seemed as if I were the criminal and not the victim. The examination, in itself a traumatic experience, was made even more traumatic by the insensitive way I was treated.—a victim

The emergency ward was full of controlled commotion.—a victim

emergency room staff is usually high, this training should be repeated periodically.

Rape victims present emergency room staffs with an enormous challenge. Some hospitals, or individuals within them, respond magnificently;[34] others remain mired in practices and attitudes that border on the unconscionable. Proper treatment of a rape victim often requires professionals trained in nursing, gynecology, psychiatry, and social work. A supportive, nonjudgmental, nonthreatening attitude is often as important as technical proficiency. Hospitals simply must recognize and respond affirmatively to their obligation to relieve suffering, not exacerbate it.

The elderly also present unique problems. What should otherwise be minor injuries can produce serious consequences in an older person. In addition, elderly victims have been schooled in another age and bring with them more traditional concepts of propriety and privacy. These victims may be overwhelmed not only by the crime but also by the pace and procedures of a busy emergency room. This will be especially so for those older persons whose experience has wrenched them from an otherwise secure pattern of life established in their later years, as well as for those who have no immediate access to close friends or family. Again, hospital staffs must act with tolerance and understanding and take the time to treat the whole patient.

Older people are more likely to break bones and dislocate hips and these injuries are very disabling. And when they are injured, there aren't any hospitals that specialize in the problems of senior citizens. We have children's hospitals and maternity hospitals.—a victim

Hospitals Recommendation 2:
Hospitals should provide emergency medical assistance to victims of violent crime without regard to their ability to pay, and collect payments from state victim compensation programs.

The Task Force is well aware that private hospitals are not charitable organizations and that they cannot be expected to provide free medical assistance to all who are in need. Many municipal hospitals are charged with serving everyone who appears at their door, regardless of their ability to pay. However, seriously injured victims must be taken to the closest hospital, whether it is private or public. These victims, in extreme physical and emotional stress, should not be turned away because it is suspected they cannot pay for needed services.

The first person we compensated was the rape victim. The rape victim doesn't even have to fill out a form. They don't have to go through that horrifying thing again, of telling what happened. The hospital directly sends a bill to our Crime Commission and, if everything is in regular order, we pay it, up to $500.— Attorney General Rufus Edmisten.

I was later taken to a hospital for an examination and treatment, and there I was met by a member of the rape crisis team. This woman provided great help and comfort to me and very much aided me in my distress.—a victim

Many victims who were questioned at length about their financial history prior to receiving treatment later discovered that the criminal who had injured them received free medical care from the state. It is necessary that prisoners be given medical attention while under the state's care; however, it may be time to reconsider whether society can ignore the innocent victims who do not themselves have the means to receive the care they need.

In states that have victim compensation programs (see Federal Executive and Legislative Recommendation 1), hospital councils and victim compensation boards should agree on policies under which hospitals would be reimbursed for the medical assistance provided to victims of crime. There are now policies in several states wherein state compensation boards negotiate with hospitals an acceptable compensation settlement that satisfies a portion of a victim's total medical indebtedness.

Hospitals Recommendation 3:

Hospitals should provide emergency room crisis counseling to victims of crime and their families.

Attention to the psychological injuries of crime victims can be just as important as the suturing of physical wounds. Most victims of violent crime are under emotional stress; if they also receive attention addressed to this aspect of their experience, they will recover more quickly and more completely.

Most modern hospitals are complete health care facilities with multidisciplinary staffs. Because of this, and because the hospital is often the first safe haven away from the crime scene, it is a logical and appropriate setting for initial crisis intervention. In some hospitals, psychiatric, social service, and chaplaincy staffs already provide crisis intervention in the emergency room.[35] This should be available on a 24-hour basis for crime victims and their families (see Appendix 2).

Health care centers have at their disposal the expertise and the trained and dedicated professionals to provide this vital service. If they truly are to be centers of healing they must recognize their obligation to those victims who need their care.

Hospitals Recommendation 4:
Hospitals should encourage and develop direct liaison
with all victim assistance and social service agencies.

No hospital can meet all the diverse needs that crime victims suddenly present. However, because hospital staffs are among the first to encounter victims of violent crime, they are in a unique position to help make these victims aware of other services available to them.[36] In attempting to cope with the stresses caused by crime, even victims themselves may not recognize some of their needs. Health care professionals can provide an important service by identifying individual victim's needs and directing the victim to appropriate assistance.

Such service presupposes an informed staff. Hospital administrators should encourage their social service or other departments both to seek out and disseminate this information and to cooperate with other service providers in the community. By such cooperation, the hospital can meet those needs it is best qualified to address and yet avoid duplicating services that are offered elsewhere.

Hospitals Recommendation 5:
Hospitals should develop, in consultation with
prosecuting agencies, a standardized rape kit for proper
collection of physical evidence, and develop a procedure
to ensure proper storage and maintenance of such
evidence until it is released to the appropriate agency.

Rape is both a medical and a legal issue. The physical evidence that offers the most convincing proof of the identity and guilt of the attacker is often recovered during the post-rape examination. Doctors and nurses who perform such examinations must ask the proper questions and acquire necessary samples in a manner that is later verifiable and amenable to productive laboratory analysis. Likewise, medical personnel must be aware of what inquiries should be made and must have at their disposal materials for evidence collection that are easily stored and readily available.

It seems unfair that after assault evidence is collected, the survivor must keep this evidence.—Marilyn E. Nessel

The best method to ensure that both medical and forensic goals are properly served is to provide an inclusive and easily used rape kit that contains a form for information gathering and materials for examination and collection of samples. Such a kit is best assembled after consultation among professionals from hospitals, police departments, prosecutors' offices, and forensic laboratories. In addition to the composition of the kit, such a group should agree on who will provide for such kits, how hospitals will acquire them, what will be done with the kit after the examination, and what agency will be responsible for the kit's proper storage. As forensic analyses advance in sophistication, proper storage becomes increasingly important.

As important as the availability of a well-designed kit is the willingness of doctors and nurses to use it. A lack of such willingness in the past has usually been attributable to a lack of awareness by medical personnel of the importance of such evidence coupled with negative experiences on those occasions in which these professionals were called to court. Prosecutors should work closely with hospital staffs to help them understand the necessity of good evidence collection and storage procedures and of the substantial contribution that attention to these procedures can make toward a successful prosecution. Attorneys must also strive to accommodate the scheduling constraints of these professionals if it should be necessary to call them as witnesses.

Recommendations for the Ministry

In hearing after hearing across the country, victims identified the religious community as a vital and largely untapped source of support for crime victims. The Government may compensate for economic loss; the state may punish; doctors may physically heal; but the lasting scars to spirit and faith are not so easily treated. Many victims question the faith they thought secure, or have no faith on which to rely. Frequently, ministers and their congregations can be a source of solace that no other sector of society can provide. It is in recognition of the unique role of the ministry that we offer the following recommendations.

1. **The ministry should recognize and address the needs of crime victims.**
2. **The ministry should develop both seminary and in-service training on the criminal justice system, the needs of victims, and ways to restore victims' spiritual and material health.**

Commentary

Ministry Recommendations 1 and 2:
(1) The ministry should recognize and minister to the needs of victims of crime; (2) The ministry should develop seminary and in-service training on the criminal justice system, the needs of victims, and ways to restore their spiritual and material health.

All too often, representatives from the religious community come to court only to give comfort, support, and assistance to the accused. This is indeed a noble endeavor, and this Task Force would not seek to discourage it. However, what we do seek, here as elsewhere, is a balance, a recognition that the victim certainly no less than the victimizer is in need of aid, comfort, and spiritual ministry. There is as great a need for a ministry to victims as there is for a ministry to prisoners.

The almost total lack of church involvement in this area is not due to any failure of charity or compas-

Many times people will trust a clergyman when they would not trust a police officer, and they will listen to us, relative to how they can be protected.—Rev. H. A. Hunderup

We were left alone to bury our daughter. More than 2,000 people attended her funeral but after the services everyone seemed to disappear. People don't know what to do or say so they stay away. Even the religious stayed away. To this day, they visit the killer and his family weekly, but for the victim's family there doesn't seem to be any time.—a victim

I found myself questioning some of the deep basic beliefs that I had grown up with. At one time they comforted me.—a victim

sion. The clergy operate under the same misconceptions and lack of information that contribute to secular insensitivity. Most people fail to meet the needs of crime victims because they do not appreciate the demands that the crime, the system, and the consequences of victimization impose. Seminary and in-service training that addresses the victim's needs is as necessary for the minister as it is for the doctor, the lawyer, or the psychologist.

There is much that can be done in addition to extending a willingness to listen and pray and give counsel; ministers and their congregations can help meet important needs. In some counties the victim/witness assistance program is operated by interfaith groups. In others, churches have undertaken extensive volunteer projects that provide 24-hour crisis counseling and court escort services in addition to emergency housing, food, and clothing. In some cities, ministers, priests, and rabbis have formed an interdenominational chaplaincy corps that is on 24-hour call to go to the scene of a crime, to the hospital, or to the homes of victims' families to ensure that this tragic information is imparted with care, and to provide the counsel and solace that they are so uniquely qualified to bring.[37]

In most of these programs, the laity as well as the clergy are deeply involved.[38] Even if there are programs offered by secular groups, or if the church is unable to cooperate in an extensive undertaking, each congregation should be mindful that every year, every congregation will have members who are victimized. It is hoped that these victims could turn to their community of faith to find understanding and support. In addition, those without faith also need help. Churches that minister only to their own meet but a small part of the problem and may discharge only a measure of their obligation.

Recommendations for the Bar

Attorneys have an obligation to their clients, to their profession, and to justice itself. They are obligated to use their expertise to guarantee that the system does not stray from the principle that lies at the heart of the law: justice for all who seek it.

1. All attorneys should recognize that they have an obligation, as officers of the court, to make certain that the justice system deals fairly with all participants in criminal litigation.
2. Prosecutors in particular should recognize their obligation to be active members of the bar at the local, state, and national levels and to represent the often unspoken needs and interests of victims.
3. Those who organize formal bar committees to deal with issues arising in the criminal justice system should ensure that the members of such groups represent a balance between the opposing parties in criminal litigation.

Commentary

The Bar Recommendation 1:
All attorneys should recognize that they have an obligation, as officers of the court, to make certain that the justice system deals fairly with all participants in criminal litigation.

Advocates for both sides of criminal litigation have a duty to give their clients the best and most effective representation possible within ethical bounds; winning at any cost is not the standard of conduct. Advocates for both sides must be constantly vigilant to protect the system from abuse. In the course of the Task Force's nationwide hearings, victims addressed five areas in which abuses occurred: plea bargaining, preliminary hearings, investigation techniques, restitution, and continuances.

Many aspects of plea bargaining, including the manner in which it is conducted, disturb victims. Although prosecutors must realistically evaluate cases, they should not agree to improperly lenient dispositions solely to dispose of cases that will be difficult, inconvenient, or unpopular to try. Defense attorneys should deal directly with the prosecutor. It is inappropriate to engage in unsolicited ex parte discussions with victims to urge them to agree to a proposed plea bargain. Neither side should converse with the court about a plea bargain without the presence of its opponent.

Advocates for both sides must avoid using preliminary hearings in ways that improperly affect victims while failing to serve the ends of justice. It is improper for the defense to use such a hearing to intimidate or embarrass a victim in the hope that he will refuse to participate further. When alternative procedures are available or the defense is willing to waive a preliminary hearing, prosecutors should not unnecessarily subject victims to such a process simply to test how they will perform as witnesses.

Attorneys must bear the responsibility of ensuring that the agents they employ behave ethically. The Task Force heard repeatedly of instances in which investigators for the defendant sought to hide their identity by telling victims "they worked for the county" or were "investigating their case," thus leading victims to believe these individuals were gathering evidence to be used against, not for, their victimizer. Such deceptive conduct should not be tolerated.

Although restitution for the losses suffered by victims should be actively pursued, victims should not be faced with a choice between recouping their losses and seeing a dangerous felon punished. Compromises that result in the dismissal of criminal charges after monetary payment should be approached with extreme caution and may not be appropriate at all in cases involving injury or large-scale fraud. No one should be given the impression that he can break the criminal law with impunity if he has resources to bargain with should he be arrested. Not only do such procedures give the impression that there is a separate system of justice for the wealthy, they also reduce substantially the deterrent value of legal sanctions. Such an approach suggests that criminals might just as well steal, because the worst that will happen is they will have to return their gains if apprehended.

I feel there should be an enforceable code of behavior with regard to the conduct of investigators from the public defender's office. An investigator misrepresented who he was and what his role in the case was. He said he was with CBI (Colorado Bureau of Investigation) and he told my father and me that if we told him our story, I wouldn't have to go to court. This is not right.—a victim

We have addressed the issue of continuances at length (see Prosecutor Recommendation 4 and Judiciary Recommendation 4) because victims find them especially vexing. Prosecutors should not seek continuances that will inconvenience the victim and jeopardize the success of prosecution to accommodate their own schedules or to avoid a difficult case. Likewise, it is not a legitimate defense tactic to delay the adjudication of a case repeatedly in the hope that witnesses will be unavailable or that their memories will fade.

Over one year since the murder—still not in trial. Feelings emerge that the longer it takes to go to trial, the ultimate decision begins to favor the defendant.—a victim

The Bar Recommendations 2 and 3:
(2) Prosecutors in particular must attend to their obligation to be active members of the bar at the local, state, and national levels and represent the often unspoken needs and interests of victims; (3) Those who organize formal bar committees to deal with issues arising in the criminal justice system should ensure that the members of such groups represent a balance between the opposing parties in criminal litigation.

In many parts of the country, prosecutors simply do not fulfill their responsibility to be active members of bar associations on behalf of crime victims. As a result, bar committees that deal with issues of criminal procedures, rules of court, legislation, jury instructions, sentencing, and the like are composed primarily or even exclusively of defense practitioners. It is difficult for any committee so composed to return recommendations or take action that gives equitable attention to the needs of victims. Yet bar committee action on jury instructions, rules of evidence, codes of ethics, and proposed substantive law often influences or determines the outcome of a case; certainly it affects the way the victim is treated in the system. Victims are entitled to a voice in these decisions, and prosecutors must see that that voice is heard.

The American Bar Association must represent those who are its members, if it operates as a democratic organization. When prosecutors pull out, you leave defense counsel.—Judge Sylvia Bacon

When bar committees that purport to represent the criminal justice community generally are organized, it is essential that their leaders ensure a balance of representative viewpoints. Lawyers are trained as advocates and, like other human beings, often operate on the principle of enlightened self-interest. Bar committees are sometimes criticized, justly, as serving or advocating only one side of an issue. Justice must not only be done, it must also be seen to be done. The bar must take care that lawyers are perceived to serve justice, not themselves.

Recommendations for Schools

Educators carry a public trust in the instruction of children. This trust means that educators are obliged to teach shared cultural values in an environment that is both scholarly and safe. When safety is not sought, when crimes go unreported, victims are unprotected and victimizers conclude that they can escape responsibility by manipulating the system. These recommendations are meant to help educators to lessen crime's impact and reduce the number of victims.

1. School authorities should develop and require compliance with guidelines for prompt reporting of violent crimes committed in schools, crimes committed against school personnel, and the possession of weapons or narcotics.
2. School authorities should check the arrest and conviction records for sexual assault, child molestation, or pornography offenses of anyone applying for work in a school, including anyone doing contract work involving regular proximity to students, and make submission to such a check a precondition for employment.
3. Educators should develop and provide courses on the problems, needs, and legal interests of victims of crime.
4. School authorities should be mindful of their responsibility to make students aware of how they can avoid being victimized by crime.

Commentary

Schools Recommendation 1:
School authorities should develop and require compliance with guidelines for prompt reporting of violent crimes committed in schools, crimes committed against school personnel, and the possession of weapons or narcotics.

School authorities must be able to respond flexibly to violations of school regulations. However, robbery, violent assaults, and the possession of dangerous drugs or weapons are more than mere transgressions of decorum. School boards should set forth guidelines that make clear to administrators, teachers, students, and parents exactly which kinds of misconduct will be handled within the school and which will be reported to the police.

School boards should also require that each school keep records of the frequency of criminal offenses. Without such records, boards have fewer ways of evaluating their administrators and cannot effectively design and direct crime prevention policies. All too frequently, authorities become aware of danger in the schools only after an outburst of violence or after the problem has become so serious and pervasive that it simply cannot be hidden any longer.

Schools Recommendation 2:
School authorities should check the arrest and conviction records for sexual assault, child molestation, or pornography offenses of anyone applying for work in a school, including anyone doing contract work involving regular proximity to students, and make submission to such a check a precondition for employment.

Administrators must take responsibility for employees who come into contact with students. Although the vast majority of those who work with children do so from the desire to help and educate youngsters, a dangerous few seek these positions so they will have ready access to a pool of victims.

The Task Force has recommended elsewhere that arrest records involving sexual assault, child molestation, or pornography be made available, without the necessity of waiver, for anyone applying for employment that would bring them into regular contact with children (see Executive and Legislative Recommendation 9). Until such legislation is passed, educators should take the initiative. It is plainly irresponsible for schools to hire individuals and take the risk that they may be accepting employment in order to victimize children. A written waiver should be required of anyone seeking employment that would put them in regular and close contact with students. This requirement would apply to teachers, counselors, administrators, coaches, bus drivers, janitors, and cafeteria staff. If these positions are filled on a contractual basis

This anguish was even greater because this man was a school bus driver who, we found out, had a record of molestation. Either the bus company didn't have access to those prison records or didn't bother checking these records, or else they just didn't care.—a victim's mother

through private enterprise, the contractors should require similar waivers and file written assurances that an appropriate investigation had been completed. Waivers would not be required of privately employed individuals performing services on an irregular and short-term basis such as schoolyard paving, building repair, and spot maintenance.

The waiver would authorize employers to obtain from local and state police, as well as from the Federal Bureau of Investigation, any record of arrest for sexual assault, child molestation, or pornography. This recommendation specifically authorizes discovery of arrest and conviction records, in recognition of the factors that militate against successful prosecution for these crimes (see Prosecutors Recommendation 8).

The Task Force recognizes that these procedures will place a burden on both schools and law enforcement agencies. However, the potential for victimization of school children and the risk of serious harm to them is substantial; this burden is, simply, one that the schools and other agencies must bear.

Schools Recommendation 3:
Educators should develop and provide courses on the problems, needs, and legal interests of victims of crime.

One-third of American households are affected by crime each year [39]—that is, a great many citizens become victims each year. Yet very little has actually been done to understand victims' reactions to crime, the long-term effects of crime on victims and those close to them, how victims' problems can best be addressed, and how social agencies can act to meet and mitigate the impact of crime.

A few pioneering studies have been conducted, but comparatively little research has been undertaken in this field. Graduate schools do not teach medical, legal, psychiatric, psychological, sociological, law enforcement, educational, or theological professionals anything about the needs of the crime victims whom they will surely encounter in their careers. This should be remedied, for many, if not most, of the problems articulated in this report stem from an insensitivity that is born of ignorance. Great care is taken to ensure that citizens are informed about the rights and concerns of the accused. This is valid and neces-

It is shocking that the study of victims' reactions, recovery, and needs is almost completely ignored in our educational system, particularly at the professional level of education.— Patricia Resick, Ph. D.

sary, but it provides only half of the education needed. Schools should also help all students understand and appreciate the needs and legal interests of victims of crimes.[40] Such education will produce better informed and educated citizens who will be more able to understand the needs of employees, neighbors, co-workers, clients, and others, including themselves, who may be victimized by crime.

Schools Recommendation 4:
School authorities should be mindful of their responsibility to make students aware of how they can avoid being victimized by crime.

All citizens, especially children, should learn how to minimize their risk of victimization. Some educators have been hesitant to provide such information for fear of alarming youngsters. This approach simply fails to recognize the seriousness of the threat posed by crime; it also fails to take into account the exposure that even the very young have to crime through television and other media. Schools should reevaluate their efforts to alert students to the dangers of crime; a brief lecture advising students not to talk to strangers is not enough. Anticrime education on this subject should be as sophisticated as the crime that poses the threat.

Recommendations for the Mental Health Community

Property damage and physical injury are readily apparent, easily understood consequences of violent crime. The psychological wounds sustained by victims of crime, and the best means of treating such injuries, are less well understood. If this severe suffering is to be relieved, mental health professionals must lead the way.

1. The mental health community should develop and provide immediate and long-term psychological treatment programs for victims of crime and their families.
2. The mental health community should establish training programs that will enable practitioners to treat crime victims and their families.
3. The mental health community should study the immediate and long-term psychological effects of criminal victimization.
4. The mental health community should work with public agencies, victim compensation boards, and private insurers to make psychological treatment readily available to crime victims and their families.
5. The mental health community should establish and maintain direct liaison with other victim service agencies.

I thought people would understand my anger, my rage, but they didn't. I found instead that the anger felt by a parent of a murdered child is too strong an emotion for our society. It is too threatening to most people, and yet if this anger is not worked through, is not channeled and is not dissipated, it will fester forever.—a victim's mother

Commentary

Mental Health Community Recommendations 1, 2, and 3:

(1) The mental health community should develop and provide immediate and long-term psychological treatment programs for victims of crime and their families; (2) The mental health community should establish training programs that will enable practitioners to treat crime victims and their families; (3) The mental health community should study the immediate and long-term psychological effects of criminal victimization.

My refuge from this isolation has been my therapist's office. Initially I returned to a therapist whom I had worked with in the past and who had been quite helpful. I found, however, that working with him now felt upsetting and harmful. I learned that not all therapists can do good work with victims of violence.—a victim

Crime victimization has been viewed as a temporary experience of physical injury that is followed by relief and recovery. With the help of mental health professionals, society is beginning to recognize that this simplistic characterization is inaccurate. Those who work with victims have had the opportunity to see that psychological effects may be profound and long-lasting.

There has been a great deal of emphasis on the evaluation and treatment of the offender; little is known of the psychological response to victimization. The application to crime victims of post-traumatic stress syndrome, articulated in the American Psychiatric Association's *Diagnostic and Statistical Manual of Mental Disorder,* [41] is an important first step. Much remains to be done, however, and certainly more research in the field is necessary. Those who undertake such inquiries must be informed not only about the kinds of crime that victims face, but also the processes of secondary victimization sustained during the investigatory and judicial process and even at the hands of well-meaning doctors, friends, counselors, and clergy. [42]

Mental Health Community Recommendation 4:
The mental health community should work with public agencies, victim compensation boards, and private insurers to make psychological treatment readily available to crime victims and their families.

The treatment of psychological injury is as important as the binding of a wound or the setting of a broken bone. The attitude that emotional therapy is an indulgence is not only uninformed but is also damaging. Crime victims often face fears and pressures that may develop into serious and prolonged emotional disturbances. These individuals must be able to get the help they so desperately need.

All too often professional care is not obtained because the victim is unable to pay for it. Professionals in this field should work closely with public agencies, as well as private industry, to ensure that needed psychological care is as readily available for victims as emergency medical care.

Mental Health Community Recommendation 5:
The mental health community should establish and maintain direct liaison with other victim service agencies.

Victims face a number of bewildering experiences beginning with the crime and extending through the court process; they should not also be bewildered when they seek psychological help. Professionals who seek to assist victims should work closely with victim service agencies in their area. Cooperation between the mental health community and victim service agencies will result in mutual benefit: agencies will profit from the mental health community's experience and professional insight and will be aware of the professional's availability for victim referral; and mental health professionals may well benefit from the experience and expertise of victim service practitioners, particularly those in the criminal justice system.

The sense of security to the family was shattered somehow. Since the incident, family functioning and relationships deteriorated, contributing to the need, even later, for additional psychiatric services. We felt isolated in our anguish and our fear.—a victim

Recommendations for the Private Sector

Crime is costly, not only to victims but also to businesses and to society as a whole. The private sector can help ease the burden carried by victims and reduce the cost of crime in several ways. Those who are victimized want to be productive in their work and responsible to their creditors; however, convalescence and court appearances may, for a time, reduce their ability to do so. If employers can be flexible in allowing absences for court appearances and medical treatment, if creditors can be more understanding in setting payment schedules, if citizens' groups can help their victimized neighbors, all will find that such forbearance will produce tangible rewards. The following recommendations offer specific suggestions for private sector action.

1. **Businesses should authorize paid administrative leave for employees who must miss work because of injuries sustained in a violent crime, and for employees who must attend court hearings.**
2. **Businesses should establish employee assistance programs for victims of crime.**
3. **Creditors should make liberal allowances for persons who are unable to make timely payments because of recent victimization.**
4. **The private sector should encourage private contributions of money and other support to victim service agencies, whether public or private.**

Commentary

Private Sector Recommendation 1:
Businesses should authorize paid administrative leave for employees who must miss work because of injuries sustained in a violent crime, and for employees who must attend court hearings.

The effects of victimization can for a time compromise an employee's ability to meet all his work-related obligations. Victims are taken away from their jobs principally for medical care and to attend court.

Crime imposes anxiety and a feeling of powerlessness; most often, victims try strenuously to put their lives back together, to get back on their feet and return to normal. The stabilizing factor of employment is often an important aid in this process. Conversely, if a victim fears the loss of a job and the economic hardship that will result, his recovery may be substantially impeded. Employers should be at least as understanding and accommodating in giving time off for medical treatment of injuries sustained in a violent crime as they would be in case of serious illness or accidents.

If criminals are to be held accountable, if crime and the cost it imposes on business and consumer alike are to be reduced, the court system must have the cooperation of victims and witnesses who will take the time and run the risk of coming forward to testify. Testifying requires that victims and witnesses leave their place of employment, or their homes, for varying lengths of time. A cooperative effort is needed here. The court system must be made more efficient; the number of required appearances must be reduced. On-call systems that would allow witnesses to remain at their jobs until they are actually needed to testify should be implemented (see Prosecutor Recommendation 5 and Judiciary Recommendation 2). Witness fees could be paid directly to employers who subsidize time off. Better scheduling of trials is also needed.

No matter how efficient the court system becomes, some sacrifices by individuals and their employers will always be necessary. Ultimately, the patience and understanding of employers will produce benefits. Hiring a new employee is expensive; training, reduced efficiency, record-keeping, and other costs make the decision to replace an employee an economic as well as a humanitarian one. The Task Force suggests that the employer who is able to bear with the transitory impositions that absences cause may ultimately profit from the work of an employee who is experienced and loyal as a result of his considerate treatment.

Private Sector Recommendation 2:
Businesses should establish employee assistance
programs for victims of crime.

Every employer has to deal with personnel difficulties from time to time. In a small business, attention is usually given on a personal basis. Larger organizations, however, often have employee assistance programs to help their workers face problems such as illness, alcohol or drug abuse, and family difficulties (see Executive and Legislative Recommendation 11 for a discussion of such programs in the government). Many businesses have crime prevention programs for their employees, and some have programs specifically designed to assist employees who have been victims of crime.[43] Both large and small businesses can profit by helping employees who have been victimized.

Private Sector Recommendation 3:
Creditors should make liberal allowances for persons who are unable to make timely payments because of recent victimization.

I was in college when I got shot. I couldn't finish the semester and I lost my $500 tuition. I was never reimbursed. The school wouldn't extend their tuition deadline for me this semester even after I explained my situation.—a victim

If a victim incurs large medical expenses or loses his job, his ability to meet his ordinary financial obligations will be affected. The Task Force urges that this impairment be recognized as transitory, that it be remembered that victims do not seek or contribute to their situation. We recognize that human patience is not infinite, but we urge that businesses be responsive to victim/witness professsionals who seek extensions for the credit payments of victims.

Private Sector Recommendation 4:
The private sector should encourage private contributions of money and other support to victim service agencies, whether public or private.

The needs of victims and the restricted budgets of programs that serve them have been discussed extensively elsewhere in this report. Business, labor, and private citizens can offer practical help in this area in much the same way that they help meet the needs of other charitable and philanthropic community enterprises. Contributions of money, goods and services, clothing, food, and shelter produce not only a tax benefit but also the reward of public good will.

Business, labor, and private citizens can make direct contributions to existing programs or supply seed money for service programs where none currently exist, either through national organizations or locally. Private sector support can take the form of in-kind contributions, such as donations of clothing or shelter for victims who have been devastated by crime; travel and hotel accommodations for victims who must return to a community for prosecution; donation of transportation or telephone equipment to facilitate 24-hour on-call services for victims; and donation of services, such as budgeting or accounting help, printing of public education brochures, medical treatment, and counseling.

Citizens' groups can become actively involved by volunteering to answer 24-hour hotlines, providing transportation and accompaniment to court, or helping a victim service agency get needed resources and access to referral services for victims with special needs. Finally, the private sector can do a great deal to assist local victim service agencies by initiating public education campaigns designed to inform people about the needs of crime victims and make them aware of the availability of services.[44]

A Proposed
Constitutional Amendment

A Proposed Amendment to the Constitution

In applying and interpreting the vital guarantees that protect all citizens, the criminal justice system has lost an essential balance. It should be clearly understood that this Task Force wishes in no way to vitiate the safeguards that shelter anyone accused of crime; but it must be urged with equal vigor that the system has deprived the innocent, the honest, and the helpless of its protection.

The guiding principle that provides the focus for constitutional liberties is that government must be restrained from trampling the rights of the individual citizen. The victims of crime have been transformed into a group oppressively burdened by a system designed to protect them. This oppression must be redressed. To that end it is the recommendation of this Task Force that the Sixth Amendment to the Constitution of the United States be augmented.

They explained the defendant's constitutional rights to the nth degree. They couldn't do this and they couldn't do that because of his constitutional rights. And I wondered what mine were. And they told me, I haven't got any.—a victim

We propose that the Amendment be modified to read as follows:

> In all criminal prosecutions the accused shall enjoy the right to a speedy and public trial, by an impartial jury of the State and district wherein the crime shall have been committed, which district shall have been previously ascertained by law, and to be informed of the nature and cause of the accusation; to be confronted with the witnesses against him; to have compulsory process for obtaining witnesses in his favor and to have the Assistance of Counsel for his defense. *Likewise, the victim, in every criminal prosecution shall have the right to be present and to be heard at all critical stages of judicial proceedings.*

We do not make this recommendation lightly. The Constitution is the foundation of national freedom, the source of national spirit. But the combined experience brought to this inquiry and everything learned during its progress affirm that an essential change must be undertaken; the fundamental rights of innocent citizens cannot adequately be preserved by any less decisive action. In this we follow Thomas Jefferson, who said: "I am not an advocate for frequent changes in laws and constitutions, but laws and institutions must go hand in hand with the progress of the human mind. As that becomes more developed, more enlightened, as new discoveries are made, new truths discovered and manners and opinions change, with the change of circumstances, institutions must advance also to keep pace with the times."

Appendices

Appendix 1: Methodology

The combined experience of the members of this Task Force in the victim and criminal justice fields is extensive. While our study was informed by our experience, we wanted to ensure that our conclusions were not the product of an insular or preconceived attitude.

We contacted professionals in those areas that touch on the victim experience, including police officers, hospital personnel, victim service providers, nurses, doctors, prosecutors, judges, private attorneys, probation and parole officers, prison and parole officials, university and law professors, researchers, mental health professionals, school teachers and administrators, members of the press, representatives from private industry, and governors, mayors, and legislators.

We compiled and analyzed as much printed material as we could acquire from governmental, academic, professional, and private sources. The synthesis of these data augments heavily the other aspects of our investigation. Crucial to our approach, however, was the concept that it was necessary to hear directly from those whose lives have been touched by crime. Therefore, we spoke at length and in great numbers with innocent people who have been victimized.

We also wanted to gain as accurate a perception as possible of what is now being done to help victims, as well as what has been tried with both successful and unsuccessful results. We found good programs in some jurisdictions and some fine first efforts in others. But one caveat must be borne in mind. Victims' problems are multifaceted, with components in almost all sectors of society. There are problems with attitudes and perceptions as well as problems with programs. Even where sound victim/witness assistance programs are in place, those victimized by crime still suffer hardship and ill treatment. Well-conceived and operated programs, as important as they are, will not provide the complete solution.

We wanted to make certain that this would not be a parochial scrutiny; to that end, we conducted hearings around the country. We decided not to hold sessions in cities that had been visited recently by other task forces or commissions dealing with criminal justice issues, because we felt we could profit by studying the information they gathered and because we wanted to give citizens from other areas the opportunity to speak to these issues. Our hearings were convened in Boston, San Francisco, Denver, St. Louis, Houston, and the District of Columbia. In addition, a great many citizens from around the nation contributed to the inquiry in personal interviews, by written submissions, by letter, and by telephone communication.

We wish to state as forcefully as possible that this Task Force does not seek to undermine in any way the essential safeguards that protect every citizen, including those accused of crime. The issues we address and the concerns we voice are not the product of any such motivation. On the contrary, it is our firm belief that every citizen must be able to expect fair treatment by his government and the system of justice that that government guarantees. What we have found is that the U.S. criminal justice system now operates in a manner that does not extend that requisite equity to all. Our sole desire is to restore a balance to the scales of justice.

This report is intended as a synthesis of information; it is not a research treatise. Research work has been undertaken by others, and their conclusions have been taken into account. Neither is this report an encyclopedic presentation of all that we have learned. We concluded that overwhelming the reader with material would undermine the impact of our recommendations. In making these recommendations we have attempted to articulate direct and workable solutions.

This report and recommendations are made to the President and the Attorney General. However, the solutions to the problems of victims will be found in federal, state, and local governmental action by executives, legislators, and judges, as well as in the actions of concerned professionals and private citizens. We have organized our report to highlight those areas of responsibility. We recognize that the implementation of these solutions must be approached with flexibility to allow for variations in local conditions. For this reason, we have intentionally refrained from mandating a single approach to implementation.

Some matters of presentation should be clarified. First, those citizens who are not direct victims of crime but who are inevitably affected by it, such as witnesses or surviving family members of homicide victims, share many of the same problems as victims, particularly with regard to their treatment by the judicial system. However, constant reference to "victims and witnesses" is stylistically cumbersome. We hope the reader will appreciate that the absence of repeated references to witnesses per se in addition to victims should not be read to imply that witnesses are not entitled to the same appropriate treatment. Similarly, both men and women are judges, lawyers, and doctors, as both are victims of crime; the traditional use of the masculine pronoun as inclusive of both genders is not meant to imply the contrary. Finally, we have tried to capture the tone of what we heard during our study by quoting victims directly; however, for the sake of their privacy and security, we have not identified victims by name if they requested anonymity.

Appendix 2: Model Victim/Witness Units

Experience has shown that the only way of ensuring that the needs of victims and witnesses are met is to have a separate unit solely dedicated to their assistance. Prosecutors, police, court personnel, and others in the criminal justice system are already overworked; moreover, these professionals may have to direct their primary efforts in ways not always consistent with response to victim needs.

Whether the victim/witness assistance unit is placed within some component of the criminal justice system or outside the system in a social service organization is best left to local determination. Excellent units are operating in police departments, prosecutors' offices, probation departments, and social service agencies. Some areas have excellent volunteer victim/witness assistance units. What is important is that the unit be well organized and staffed by dedicated personnel, that it be funded generously enough to provide comprehensive services, and that its actions be coordinated with those of agencies within the criminal justice system, private service groups, and business organizations.

The success of such units is measured by how swiftly and well they meet the needs of victims and witnesses. We have identified the needs that we consider most important, the ones that every victim witness unit should meet. A model victim/witness assistance unit should:

1. Assist every victim who reports a crime, whether or not an arrest is made.
2. Respond to the scene of the crime to make crisis counseling available. Programs that offer such services include the following: Victim/Witness Unit, Alameda County, Calif.; Victim/Witness Unit, Sacramento County, Calif.; Victim/Witness Unit, Ventura County, Calif.; Victim Information Program, Louisville, Ky.; Crime Victims Center, Minneapolis/St. Paul,

Minn.; Victim Assistance Program, Glendale, Ariz.; Victim/Witness Unit, Greenville, S.C.; Victim Services Agency, New York, N.Y., and Victim/Witness Unit, Lincoln Police Department, Lincoln, Neb.

3. Provide 24-hour telephone hotline service to victims and witnesses for assistance, particularly if threats or intimidation occur. Programs that offer such services include the following: Victim/Witness Advocate Program, Pima County, Ariz.; Crime Victims Center, Minneapolis/St. Paul, Minn.; Victim Services Division, Colorado Springs Police Department, Colorado Springs, Colo.; Victim/Witness Unit, Indianapolis, Ind.; Victim/Witness Unit, Evanston, Ill.; Victim/Witness Unit, Scottsdale, Ariz.; and Victim/Witness Unit, Ft. Lauderdale, Fla.

4. Make emergency monetary aid available to help needy victims make their homes secure, replace such things as glasses and hearing aids, and buy food and other necessities. Programs that offer such services include the following: Victim/Witness Advocate Program, Pima County, Ariz.; Crime Victims Center, Minneapolis/St. Paul, Minn.; Victim Services Agency, New York, N.Y.; Victim/Witness Unit, Chester, Pa.; Victim/Witness Unit, Dade County, Fla.; and Victim/Witness Unit, Ft. Lauderdale, Fla.

5. Refer victims to appropriate social service and victim compensation programs and assist in filling out forms for compensation. Programs that offer such services include the following: Victim/Witness Assistance Unit, Boulder, Colo.; Victim/Witness Assistance Center, Clark County, Nev.; Victim Assistance Project, Multnomah County, Ore.; Victim /Witness Assistance Unit, St. Louis, Mo.; Victim/Witness Unit, Sacramento County, Calif.; Victim/Witness Unit, Ventura County, Calif.; Victim/Witness Unit, Honolulu, Hi.; Victim/Witness Unit, King County, Wash.; Victim/Witness Unit, Denver, Colo.; and Crime Victims Center, Minneapolis/St. Paul, Minn.

6. Educate the public about the operation of the criminal justice system and the way it treats victims. Public education is a major focus of the Boston area Victim/Witness programs.

7. Assist in prompt return of victim's property. Programs that offer such services include the following: Project Turnaround, Milwaukee, Wisc.; Victim/Witness Unit, Alameda County, Calif.; and Victim/Witness Unit, Sacramento County, Calif.

8. Notify the victim of progress of the investigation, the defendant's arrest, subsequent bail determination and status of the case as it proceeds through the system. Programs that offer such services include the following: Victim/ Witness Assistance Unit, Boulder, Colo.; Victim/Witness Assistance Center, Clark County, Nev.; Victim Assistance Project, Multnomah County, Ore.; Victim/Witness Assistance Unit, St. Louis, Mo.; Victim/Witness Unit, Sacramento County, Calif.; Victim/Witness Unit, Ventura County, Calif.; Victim/Witness Unit, Honolulu, Hi.; Victim/Witness Unit, King County, Wash.; Victim/Witness Unit, Denver, Colo.; and Crime Victims Center, Minneapolis/St. Paul, Minn.

9. Assist victims in making appropriate input on the following: bail determinations, continuances, plea bargaining, dismissals, sentencing, restitution and parole hearings. Programs that offer such assurance on bail determinations include: Victim/ Witness Unit, Chicago, Ill., and Victim/Witness Assistance Unit, St. Louis, Mo.; on sentencing, Victim Information Unit, Louisville, Ky.; and on parole, Victim/Witness Unit, Muskogee, Okla.

10. Consult with victims and witnesses to facilitate the setting of convenient hearing dates. Programs that offer such services include the following: Victim/Witness Assistance Unit, Boulder, Colo.; Victim/Witness Assistance Center, Clark County, Nev.; Victim Assistance Project, Multnomah County, Ore.; Victim/Witness Assistance Unit, St. Louis, Mo.; Victim/Witness

Unit, Sacramento County, Calif.; Victim/Witness Unit, Ventura County, Calif.; Victim/Witness Unit, Honolulu, Hi.; Victim/Witness Unit, King County, Wash.; Victim/Witness Unit, Denver, Colo.; and Crime Victims Center, Minneapolis/St. Paul, Minn.

11. Implement a victim/witness on-call system. Programs that offer such services include the following: Victim/Witness Unit, Denver, Colo.; Project Turnaround, Milwaukee, Wisc.; Victim/Witness Unit, Peoria, Ill.; Victim Information Unit, Louisville, Ky.; Victim Services Agency, New York, N.Y.; Victim/Witness Unit, Ventura County, Calif.; Victim/Witness Unit, Greenville, S.C.; and Victim/Witness Unit, Adams County, Colo.

12. Intercede with the employers or creditors of victims or witnesses. Programs that offer such services include the following: Victim/Witness Unit, Greenville, S.C.; Victim Assistance Project, Multnomah County, Ore.; and Victim/ Witness Unit, Peoria, Ill.

13. Assist the elderly and handicapped in arranging transportation to and from court. Programs that offer such services include the following: Jamaica Service Program for Older Adults, Jamaica, N.Y.; Victim/Witness Unit, Clark County, Nev., and Victim Assistance Project, Multnomah County, Ore.

14. Provide a translator service. Programs that offer such services include the following: Victim/Witness Unit, Essex County, Mass.; Victim Services Agency, New York, N.Y., and Victim/Witness Unit, Dade County, Fla.

15. Coordinate efforts to ensure that victims have a secure place to wait before testifying. Programs that offer such services include the following: Victim/Witness Unit, Ventura County, Calif.; Victim/Witness Unit, Portsmouth, Va.; Victim Services Agency, New York, N.Y., and Project Turnaround, Milwaukee, Wisc.

16. Provide counseling or companionship during court appearances when appropriate. Programs that offer such services include the following: Victim/Witness Assistance Unit, Boulder,

Colo.; Victim/Witness Assistance Center, Clark County, Nev.; Victim Assistance Project, Multnomah County, Ore.; Victim/Witness Assistance Unit, St. Louis, Mo.; Victim/Witness Unit, Sacramento County, Calif.; Victim/Witness Unit, Ventura County, Calif.; Victim/Witness Unit, Honolulu, Hi.; Victim/Witness Unit, King County, Wash.; Victim/Witness Unit, Denver, Colo.; and Crime Victims Center, Minneapolis/St. Paul, Minn.

Appendix 3: Witnesses Before the President's Task Force on Victims of Crime

Witnesses at each hearing are listed according to the order in which they appeared before the Task Force.

Hearing in Washington, D.C., September 14–15, 1982

William French Smith, Attorney General of the United States

John Heinz, U.S. Senator, State of Pennsylvania

Evelyn Blackwell, crime victim

Marlene A. Young, Executive Director, National Organization for Victim Assistance

D. Lowell Jensen, Assistant Attorney General, Criminal Division, U.S. Department of Justice

George Sunderland, Senior Coordinator, American Association of Retired Persons

Edwin C. Meese, counselor to the President

Rufus L. Edmisten, Attorney General, State of North Carolina

Lynn A. Marks, Executive Director, Women Organized Against Rape, Philadelphia, Pa.

Dorothea Morefield, crime victim

Morton Bard, Professor of Psychology, City College of New York

Crime victim (name withheld on request)

Crime victim (name withheld on request)

Deborah P. Kelly, Assistant Professor, University of Maryland

Howard Safir, Assistant Director for Operations, U.S. Marshal's Service

David L. Armstrong, Commonwealth's Attorney, 30th Judicial District, Louisville, Ky.

Reggie Walton, Judge of the Superior Court of the District of Columbia

Stanley S. Harris, U.S. Attorney for the District of
Columbia
Rev. H. A. Hunderup, Portsmouth, Va., Police
Department Chaplaincy Corps
Lieut. R. K. Gaddis, Portsmouth, Va., Police
Department
Kathy Musser, crime victim
Ann W. Burgess, D.N.Sc., Associate Director of Nurs-
ing Research, Boston City Hospital
Kenneth Lanning, Special Agent, Behavioral Science
Unit, Federal Bureau of Investigation
Michael Watson, Special Agent, Federal Bureau of
Investigation
Daniel J. Popeo, General Counsel, Washington Legal
Foundation
Sylvia Bacon, Judge of the Superior Court of the
District of Columbia, and Immediate Past
Chairperson, American Bar Association Section on
Criminal Justice
Laurie O. Robinson, Director, American Bar
Association Section on Criminal Justice
Susan W. Hillenbrand, Victim/Witness Assistance
Project, American Bar Association Section on
Criminal Justice
John Walsh, crime victim
Joyce Thomas, R.N., Director, Child Protection Unit,
Children's Hospital National Medical Center,
Washington, D.C.
David Lloyd, Attorney-at-Law, Child Protection Unit,
Children's Hospital National Medical Center,
Washington, D.C.
Gary D. Gottfredson, Director, Program in
Delinquency and School Environments, Johns
Hopkins University
Chiquita Bass, crime victim
James Ahrens, Law Enforcement Specialist
Susan Salasin, Chairperson, Committee on the Mental
Health Services Needs of Victims of Violence, World
Federation for Mental Health
Rev. Herman Head, Prison Fellowship

Hearing in Boston, Mass., September 21–22, 1982:

William F. Weld, U.S. Attorney, Boston, Mass.
Kevin M. Burke, District Attorney, Essex County, Mass.
Margaret Grogan, crime victim
Barbara E. Gray, Massachusetts State Representative
Mary Jo Zingarelli, crime victim
Lucy N. Friedman, Ph.D., Director, Victim Service Agency, New York City
Rev. Neal J. DeStefano, S.J., Chaplain, Quincy, Mass., Police Department; Chaplain, Boston City Hospital
Ronald C. Zweibel, President, National Association of Crime Victim Compensation Boards
Daniel McGillis, Ph.D., Center for Criminal Justice, Harvard Law School; Consultant, Abt Associates Inc.
Patricia Smith, Abt Associates Inc.
Sally Bowie, Lic.S.W., Director, Rape Crisis Intervention Program, Beth Israel Hospital, Boston, Mass.
Robert Dumond, Director, District Attorney's Victim/ Witness Assistance, Northern Essex County, Mass.
George Carroll, crime victim
Julio Vargus, crime victim
Mrs. Alan Dixon, crime victim
David Lowenberg, Director, Victim/Witness Program, Pima County, Ariz.
Lorna Bernhard, R.N., B.S., Head Nurse, Pediatric Emergency Room, Boston City Hospital
Susan J. Kelley, R.N., M.S., Nurse Coordinator, Massachusetts State Office of Emergency Medical Services
William G. Robinson, Massachusetts State Representative
Barbara Kaplan, crime victim
Karen McLaughlin, Director, Victim Assistance Program, Essex County, Massachusetts District Attorney's Office
Richard M. Cook, crime victim
Charles Austin, Reporter, WBZ Television News
David J. Millet, Lieutenant, Police Department, Marblehead, Mass.
Michael Levitt, Reporter, WNEV Television News

Emily Chandler, R.N., M.S., Director of Psychiatric Services, Boston Department of Health and Hospitals
Maureen Ellis, R.N., M.S., Psychiatric Clinical Specialist for Pediatric Nursing, Boston City Hospital
Martin A. Walsh, Cochairperson, Greater Boston Civil Rights Coalition
Joseph Feaster, Jr., Cochairperson, Greater Boston Civil Rights Coalition
Dennis J. Roberts II, Attorney General, State of Rhode Island
Sister Annunciata Bethell, Director, Bedford Park Multi-Service Center for Senior Citizens Inc., Bronx, N.Y.
Crime victim (name withheld on request)
Amy Singer, Director, Victim/Witness Program, Middlesex County, Massachusetts District Attorney's Office
Crime victim (name withheld on request)
Robert Grayson, crime victim; Chairman, New Jersey Council on Crime victims
Gail Pisarcik, R.N., M.S., C.S., Coordinator, Emergency Services for Rape Victims, Massachusetts General Hospital
Janet Yassen, M.S.W., Lic.S.W., Clinician, Cambridge-Somerville, Massachusetts Mental Health & Retardation Center; Member, Boston Area Rape Crisis Center
Margaret Kelly, crime victim
Rose Cropper, crime victim
Rosemary Kelly, Coordinator, Victim/Witness Assistance, Suffolk County, Massachusetts District Attorney's Office
Newman Flanagan, District Attorney, Suffolk County, Mass.

Hearing in San Francisco, Calif., September 30— October 1, 1982

Dianne Feinstein, Mayor, City of San Francisco
Michael Salerno, crime victim
Harriet Salerno, crime victim

Marilyn Hall Patel, U.S. District Judge, San Francisco, Calif.
Annette Carlson, crime victim
Elizabeth Stewart Carlson, crime victim
George Nicholson, Coauthor, California Victim Bill of Rights
Donald McGrath, II, Attorney-at-Law
Merrill J. Schwartz, Attorney-at-Law
Thomas Peters, Ph.D., Director, Office of Forensic Services, San Francisco Department of Public Health
Margaret Reiss, M.S.W, Center for Special Problems, San Francisco, Department of Public Health
Linda Eberth, M.S.W, Sexual Trauma Services, San Francisco Department of Public Health
Marge Harrer, Ph.D., Child/Adolescent Sexual Assault Resource Center, San Francisco General Hospital
Nancy J. Bowman, crime victim
Robert P. Owens, Chief of Police, Oxnard, Calif.
Robert L. Buhrig, Corporate Security Manager, Southland Corporation
Beth P. Doolittle, Program Coordinator, Rape Crisis Center, Marin County, Calif.
John J. Meehan, District Attorney, Alameda County, Calif.
George Bush, Vice President of the United States
Daphne D. Moore, crime victim
Anna Foy, crime victim
Mary Nordby, crime victim
Carol Corrigan, Professor of Law
James Rowland, Chief Probation Officer, Fresno County, Calif.
Lucy Berliner, M.S.W., Harborview Medical Center, Seattle, Wash.
Douglas Cunningham, Executive Director, California Office of Criminal Justice Planning
Mary Miller, crime victim
Veronica C. Zecchini, Program Coordinator, Victim/Witness Program, District Attorney's Office, Sacramento County, Calif.
Harold O. Boscovich, Director, Victim/Witness Assistance Bureau, District Attorney's office, Alameda County, Calif.
Joseph Yomtov, Director, Santa Clara, California Victim/Witness Program

Anne Daley, Director, Victim/Witness Assistance
Program, San Francisco, California District
Attorney's Office
Frank Jordan, Lieutenant, Crime Prevention Division,
San Francisco Police Department
Mark Forrester, Director, Senior Escort Outreach
Program, San Francisco Police Department
Gwendolyn Dillworth-Battle, Executive Director, San
Francisco SAFE Crime Prevention Project
Elvis Regalia, crime victim
Edith Benay, crime victim

Hearing in Denver, Colo., October 5–6, 1982

Robert N. Miller, U.S. Attorney for the District of
Colorado
Robert Hedges, crime victim
Dale Tooley, District Attorney, Denver, Colo.
Mary E. Taitt, crime victim
Eugene Taitt, crime victim
Barbara Chaffee, crime victim
Bette H. North, Director, Victim/Witness Unit,
Adams County, Colo.
Roy Ter Horst, crime victim
Barbara Kendall, Director, Victim/Witness Unit,
Boulder County, Colo.
Kathleen Skelton, crime victim
Crime victim (name withheld on request)
Crime victim (name withheld on request)
Crime victim (name withheld on request)
Bea McPherson, Director, Society's League Against
Molesters (SLAM), Littleton, Colo.
Irving Prager, Professor, LaVerne College of Law,
Calif.
Dorothy Minkle, crime victim
Priscilla Conrad, Director, Victim/Witness Unit,
Denver, Colo.
Edith Surgan, crime victim; Chairman, New Mexico
Crime Victim Reparations Board and President,
Crime Victims Assistance Organization
Crime victim (name withheld on request)
Anne Compton, Boulder County Rape Crisis Center,
Boulder, Colo.

Phyllis Wisse, crime victim
Sue Conley, crime victim
Richard D. Lamm, Governor, State of Colorado
Pat Wyka, Coordinator, Victim Services Division,
Colorado Springs Police Department, Colo.
Crime victim (name withheld on request)
Crime victim (name withheld on request)
Dr. Lenore Walker, psychologist
Melodye Feldman, Colorado Domestic Violence
Coalition
Jerry Williams, Chief of Police, Arvada, Colo.
Roberta Conway, crime victim

Hearing in St. Louis, Mo., October 13–14, 1982

Hyman Eisenberg, crime victim
Crime victim (name withheld on request)
Carol Vittert, community volunteer
Harold Tuthill, crime victim
Fern Y. Ferguson, M.S.W., Director, Social Services
Department, St. Mary's Hospital, E. St. Louis, Ill.
B. David Brooks, Ph.D., Director, Safe Schools—
Safe Streets Project, Thomas Jefferson Research
Center, Los Angeles, Calif.
Frank M. Ochberg, M.D., Mental Health Center, St.
Lawrence Hospital, Lansing, Mich.
Justice William Callow, Supreme Court, State of
Wisconsin
Linda Jackson, crime victim
Thomas Amberg, Staff Writer—St. Louis Globe-
Democrat, St. Louis, Mo.
Pamela Klein, Director, Rape and Sexual Abuse Care
Center, Southern Illinois University
Betty Jane Spencer, crime victim
Ernest Allen, Executive Director, Criminal Justice
Commission, Louisville-Jefferson County, Ky.
Buzz Westfall, Prosecuting Attorney, St. Louis
County, Mo.
Betsy Munro, Executive Director, Victim Service
Council, St. Louis County, Mo.
Marjorie Susman, community volunteer
Louise Ann Bauschard, A.C.S.W., Executive Director,
Women's Self Help Center, St. Louis, Mo.
Ginny Davis, crime victim

Ed Stout, Executive Director, Aid for Victims of
Crime, Inc., St. Louis, Mo.
Rose Flynn, crime victim
Suzanne F. Valdez, crime victim
Judy Miller, crime victim
Patricia A. Resick, Ph.D., Department of
Psychology, University of Missouri—St. Louis
Judy K. Raker, Assistant Circuit Attorney, City of St.
Louis
Robert L. Toms, Board Member, Hollywood,
California Presbyterian Medical Center
Diane S. Kerckhoff, community volunteer
Marilyn Lane, Victim/Witness Unit, Circuit
Attorney's Office, St. Louis, Mo.
Crime victim (name withheld on request)
Ricky Smith, crime victim
Linda Riekes, Director, Law and Education Project,
St. Louis Public Schools, Mo.
Delphine McClellan, Partners Against Crime
Together, St. Louis, Mo.
Ann Slaughter, Partners Against Crime Together, St.
Louis, Mo.

Hearing in Houston, Tex., October 19, 1982

Ann Keith, crime victim
Marilyn Nessel, Houston Area Women's Center
Nancy Owen, crime victim
Maureen McGrath, social worker, The Methodist
Hospital, Houston, Tex.
Ted Poe, Judge, District Court of Harris County,
Houston, Tex.
Suzanne McDaniel, Director, The Witness Office,
Harris County District Attorney's Office, Houston,
Tex.
Robert Delong, Attorney-at-Law
Robert J. Rubel, Ph.D., Center for Improved
Learning Environments, San Marcos, Tex.
Raymond H. C. Teske, Professor, Criminal Justice
Center, Sam Houston State University
Robert Reiff, psychologist
Thomas Taitt, administrative assistant, Clark County,
Nev. District Attorney's Office
Deborah Emm, crime victim

Notes

1. The State of Pennsylvania has codified this privilege in 42 Pa. C.S.A. § 5945.1, "Confidential communications to sexual assault counselors."

2. U.S. Department of Justice, National Institute of Justice, *Pretrial Release: A National Evaluation of Practices and Outcomes* (Washington, D.C.: U.S. Government Printing Office, 1981); John S. Goldcamp, *Two Classes of Accused* (Cambridge: Ballinger Publishing Co., 1979); U.S. Department of Justice, National Institute of Corrections, *Bail Decision-making: A Study of Policy Guidelines.* (Washington, D.C. U.S. Government Printing Office, 1981).

3. Elizabeth Gaynes, "Typology of state laws which permit the consideration of danger in the pretrial release decision." Paper available from the Pretrial Services Resource Center, Washington, D.C. (May 1982).

4. People *v.* De Fore, 242 N.Y. 13, 150 N.E., 585, 587 (1926).

5. United States *v.* Janis, 428 U.S. 433, 449 n. 21 (1976); Malcolm Richard Wilkey, "The constitutional alternatives to the exclusionary rule," *South Texas Law Journal,* vol. 23, no. 3, p. 5 (December 1982).

6. U.S. Department of Health, Education and Welfare, National Institute of Education, *Violent Schools—Safe Schools: The Safe School Study Report to the Congress* (Washington, D.C.: U.S. Government Printing Office, 1978).

7. We are well aware that this recommendation may conflict with existing state and federal laws concerning the maintenance and dissemination of arrest histories as these laws are presently drafted. We firmly believe, however, that it is necessary to create exceptions in these statutes to provide for this information to be collected and dis-

seminated to private organizations or governmental entities that will be hiring adults to supervise or work near children. This is a very narrow exception and potential employees who fear disclosure of their records always have the option of not applying for jobs in child-related fields. The safety of children is paramount; every reasonable step to protect them must be taken.

8. American Bar Association, Section of Criminal Justice, *Victim/Witness Legislation: Considerations for Policymakers* (U.S. Department of Justice, Law Enforcement Assistance Administration Grant #80-CJ-AX-0099). See especially chapter 2.

9. Title II of Public Law 91-616, "Comprehensive Alcohol Abuse and Alcohol Prevention, Treatment and Rehabilitation Act of 1970," as amended by Public Law 93-282; Title IV of Public Law 92-255, "Drug Abuse Office and Treatment Act of 1972," as amended by Public Law 93-282.

10. We are indebted to the Attorney General's Task Force on Violent Crime for recommending that a thorough update of American crime victim compensation programs be conducted. The completed study has served as the cornerstone of our inquiry in this area. (U.S. Department of Justice, National Institute of Justice, *Compensating Victims of Crime: An Analysis of American Programs,* report prepared by Abt Associates Inc., October 1982).

11. Ronald Zweibel, President of the National Association of Crime Victim Compensation Programs, testified that "virtually all state crime victim compensation programs have financial problems. . . ." (Boston hearing, September 21, 1982).

12. *Compensating Victims of Crime,* p. 92.

13. *Ibid.*, p. 86.

14. Testimony of Amy Singer, Boston hearing, September 22, 1982.

15. *Compensating Victims of Crime,* pp. 135–136.

16. *Ibid.*, p. 136.

17. Testimony of a crime victim (name withheld on request), San Francisco hearing, September 30, 1982.

18. *Compensating Victims of Crime,* p. 87

19. David A. Lowenberg, "An integrated victim services model," in *Perspectives on Crime Victims,* Burt Galaway and Joe Hudson, eds. (St. Louis, Missouri: The C.V. Mosby Company, 1981).

20. The United States Attorney's Offices in Washington, D.C., and Colorado currently have victim/witness assistance programs. The D.C. program, however, is based in the District of Columbia Superior Court, which handles local, not federal, prosecutions.

21. Payton *v.* United States, —F.2d— (5th Cir. July 1, 1982) *(en banc),* 51 U.S.L.W. 2028 (July 13, 1982); Rieser *v.* District of Columbia, 563 F.2d 462 (D.C. Cir. 1977), *aff'd en banc,* 580 F.2d 647 (1978); Semler *v.* Psychiatric Inst., 538 F.2d 121 (4th Cir. 1976); Grimm *v.* Arizona Bd. of Pardons & Paroles, 115 Ariz. 260, 267, 564 P.2d 1227, 1234 (1977) *(en banc);* Martinez *v.* California, 444 U.S. 277 (1980); Pate *v.* Alabama Bd. of Pardons & Paroles, 409 F. Supp. 478 (M.D. Ala. 1976); Thompson *v.* County of Alameda, 27 Cal. 3d 741, 614 P.2d 728, 167 Cal. Rptr. 70 (1980); Lloyd *v.* State, 251 N.W. 2d 551 (Iowa 1977).

22. Payton v. United States, *supra.*

23. Martin Symonds, "The 'Second Injury' to Victims," *Evaluation and Change,* Special Issue 1980. Dr. Symonds developed training programs for police entitled, "Psychological first-aid for victims of crime."

24. Several law enforcement agencies across the country have already instituted training programs emphasizing stress management and crisis intervention. These programs not only assist the officer in developing more sensitive treatment of victims, they also are intended to help the officer develop more cooperative and satisfied witnesses who are able to give more complete and accurate information. (Testimony by James Ahrens, Washington hearing, September 15, 1982, and by Robert Owens, San Francisco hearing, September 30, 1982).

25. Testimony by Rev. H. A. Hunderup, Washington hearing, September 15, 1982.

26. American Bar Association, Section of Criminal Justice, *Reducing Victim/Witness Intimidation: A Package and "How to do it" Suggestions for Implementing the ABA Victim/witness Intimidation Recommendations* (Washington, D.C., 1981); Robert C. Davis, Victor Russell, and Frances Kunreuther, *The Role of the Complaining Witness in an Urban Criminal Court* (New York: Victim Services Agency, 1980); Elizabeth Connick, *Witness Intimidation: An Examination of the Criminal Justice System's Response to the Problem* (New York: Victim Services Agency, 1982).

27. Testimony by Bea McPherson and Irving Prager, Denver hearing, October 5, 1982. Escalation of behavior occurs as molesters learn that they can victimize children with impunity, because official sanctions are imposed so infrequently.

28. "Prison Industry: No longer Only So Much Soft Soap," *Corrections Compendium,* Vol. V., No. 6 (December 1980).

29. Testimony by Joyce Thomas, Washington hearing, September 15, 1982.

30. Testimony by Bea McPherson and Irving Prager, Denver hearing, October 5, 1982, as well as numerous discussions with other experts in this area.

31. The State of Wisconsin *v.* Snodgrass, Circuit Court of Crawford County, Wisconsin, Case No. 80CF51.

32. Testimony by Irving Prager and Bea McPherson, Denver hearing, October 5, 1982. Therapists report that one of the major reasons for therapy's failure to modify this behavior is an unwillingness on the part of molesters to change their conduct.

33. Bradley *v.* Fairfax, 634 F.2d 1126 (8th Cir. 1980); United States ex. rel. Sperling *v.* Fitzpatrick, 426 F.2d 1161 (2d Cir. 1970); Lewis *v.* U.S. Parole Commission, 448 F. Supp. 1327 (E.D. Mich. 1978); J. Cole, "The Exclusionary Rule in Probation and Parole Revocation Proceedings: Some Observations on Deterrence and the 'Imperative of Judicial Integrity.'" 52 Chicago-Kent L. Rev. 21 (1975).

34. Beth Israel Hospital in Boston, for example, provides training to emergency room staff, interns, and other hospital personnel on the special needs and appropriate treatment for rape victims. The medical interns spend several months providing counseling to rape victims.

35. For example, 24-hour crisis intervention for crime victims is provided by psychiatric nurses at Boston City Hospital, Boston, Mass.

36. Many cities have initiated multi-agency coordinating committees to address the needs of victims

of sexual violence. Hospital personnel have been active members of these committees. A noteworthy achievement of such coordination is the development of a specialized treatment center for all victims of sexual assault at St. Louis City Hospital, St. Louis, Mo.

37. In Portsmouth, Va., for example, a corps of 15 area clergy work with the police department to assist crime victims. They are on 24-hour call and respond with the police to the crime scene. The police in turn contribute some funds and a vehicle to the chaplaincy corps, allowing the corps to provide emergency assistance to victims in need.

38. The Bedford Park Multi-Service Center for Senior Citizens in the Bronx, N.Y., is run by Sister Annunciata Bethell and staffed by volunteers from the church and from the local community. The center combines crime prevention for seniors with 24-hour services for those who have been victims of crime.

39. U.S. Department of Justice, Bureau of Justice Statistics, *Households Touched by Crime, 1981* (Washington, D.C.: U.S. Government Printing Office, 1982).

40. The St. Louis, Mo., public school district includes instruction on the needs and legal interests of crime victims as part of its law-related education curriculum.

41. American Psychiatric Association; *Diagnostic and Statistical Manual of Mental Disorders,* Third Edition (1980).

42. The San Francisco Public Health Department provides immediate and long-term psychological treatment for crime victims, staff training, and research on criminal victimization.

140

43. American Society for Industrial Security report on private sector efforts to assist victims of crime, submitted to the President's Task Force on Victims of Crime, November 1982.

44. Victim/witness assistance programs are receiving support from the private sector in many areas throughout the country. For example, the circuit attorney in the city of St. Louis, Mo., sets an annual minimum amount to be raised from local businesses to pay for services he provides through his victim/witness assistance unit. The business community has responded positively. The Dade County, Fla., government accepts private contributions for the local victim/witness program. In Pima County, Ariz., the countywide victim/witness assistance program receives contributions for its public education materials. For example, a recent booklet on the particular needs of bank robbery victims was paid for by local banks. In Clark County, Nev., the Citizens Committee for Victim Rights is made up of local businesses and community organizations. This committee raises funds for victim/witness services and also makes decisions on how the money should be spent. The Victim/Witness Assistance Service of Chester County, Pa., receives almost its entire budget from private contributions.

Some national organizations have encouraged their local membership groups to use their money to support existing victim/witness programs or to develop new programs. These organizations include the National Council of Jewish Women, the General Federation of Women's Clubs, the Kiwanis, and the Association of Junior Leagues.

Many victim/witness programs rely heavily on volunteers from the private sector. The Colorado Springs Police Department's Senior Victim Assistance team for elderly crime victims is staffed by volunteers, many of whom are senior citizens themselves; the Victim Services Council in St. Louis County, Mo., relies heavily on local volunteers; and in Minneapolis/St. Paul, Minn., the Crime Victims Center recruits and trains volunteers to answer the 24-hour crisis hotline for crime victims in need.

Biographies

Lois Haight Herrington is a practicing attorney who has served as a deputy district attorney, probation officer, and counselor in Juvenile Hall in California. Ms. Herrington previously maintained a private law practice. She has also been a member of the Alameda County Women's Coalition on Domestic Violence, the Contra Costa County Child Development Council, the California Sexual Assault Investigators Conference and Juvenile Justice Conference. Additionally, Ms. Herrington has served as a coordinator for Probation and Courts for Domestic Violence Diversion programs and an instructor for Drug Diversion and Education Program, and a volunteer vocational counselor at a California high school.

Garfield Bobo is a Court Assistant for the Supreme Court of New York. He has also held positions as President of the Bedford-Stuyvesant Improvements Association and as a member of the Urban League of Greater New York. Previously, Mr. Bobo has worked with the Supreme Court Criminal Justice Division in Kings County, N.Y., the State of New York Division of Housing and Community Renewal, and the Board of Elections of the City of New York.

Frank Carrington is Executive Director of the Victims Assistance Legal Organization (VALOR) in Virginia. An attorney and author, Mr. Carrington also is currently chairman of the Victim Committee of the American Bar Association, a Director of the National Organization for Victims Assistance, a member of California's Attorney General's Commission on Victims. He also served on President Reagan's transition committee on Law Enforcement, Justice, and Victims, and the Attorney General's Task Force on Violent Crime. He has authored several books, including *The Victim.*

James P. Damos is the Chief of Police for University City, Mo. He is also President of the International Association of Chiefs of Police. Chief Damos' other activities have included: Vice Chairman of the Law Enforcement Police Committee of the Regional Justice Information System, the Governor's Task Force on Rape Prevention, the National Advisory Board Crusade Against Crime, and the Governor's Commission on Crime.

Doris L. Dolan is the founder and President of Laws at Work in California. She is also Project Director for the National Education Institute. Some of Ms. Dolan's other actitivies have included appointments to the Los Angeles Greater Urban Coalition, Law and Justice Task Force, the National Council on Criminal Justice, the California Arson Task Force, and the President's Crime Victims Advisory Committee.

Kenneth O. Eikenberry was elected Attorney General of the State of Washington in 1980. Prior to election to this office, Mr. Eikenberry has served as an elected representative to the Washington State House of Representatives, a special agent with the Federal Bureau of Investigation, and a deputy prosecuting attorney for King County, Washington.

Robert J. Miller is the District Attorney of Clark County, Nev. He is also the founder of the Citizens Committee on Victims Rights, and Special Advisor to the National Organization for Victim Assistance on Victims Rights. Mr. Miller has served as Vice President of the National District Attorneys Association and was Co-chairman of Victims Rights Week in 1982. Mr. Miller has also served as a Clark County Justice of the Peace (Criminal Magistrate Court) and a deputy sheriff of Las Vegas, Nev. and Los Angeles, Calif.

Marion G. (Pat) Robertson is President of the Christian Broadcasting Network, Inc. (CBN) of Virginia Beach, Va., and host of the Network's television program "The 700 Club." An attorney, a clergyman, and an author of many books, the Reverend Robertson is also founder and chancellor of CBN University, and a director of National Religious Broadcasters and the United Bank of Virginia. He has also produced "Pat Robertson's Perspective,"—a report and analysis of world affairs.

Stanton E. Samenow is President of the Center for Responsible Living in Alexandria, Va. He also serves as an Assistant Professor of Psychiatry at George Washington University School of Medicine in Washington, D.C., as a member of the President's Law Enforcement Task Force, and maintains a private practice in clinical psychology. In addition, Dr. Samenow is a psychological consultant to the Federal Bureau of Investigation and many other public and private sector organizations throughout the United States. He is co-author of the three-volume set, *The Criminal Personality.*

Terry Russell is an Assistant U.S. Attorney for the District of Columbia, where he has served as the Deputy Director of Superior Court Operations. He was the Deputy Director of the Attorney General's Task Force on Violent Crime, and is a member of the Victims Committee of the Criminal Justice Section of the American Bar Association. Mr. Russell initiated the first victim/witness assistance unit within a U.S. Attorney's Office.